11+

MATHS

Book Five

Stephen C. Curran

edited by
Anne-Marie Choong
Tandip Singh Mann

This book belongs to:

....

Accelerated Education Publications Ltd.

Contents

Chapter Sixteen
PERIMETER, AREA & VOLUME

Mensuration describes the process of Measuring Shapes.

1. Perimeter

Perimeter is the Distance all the way round the outside of a Shape. Example:

What is the Perimeter of this Rectangle?

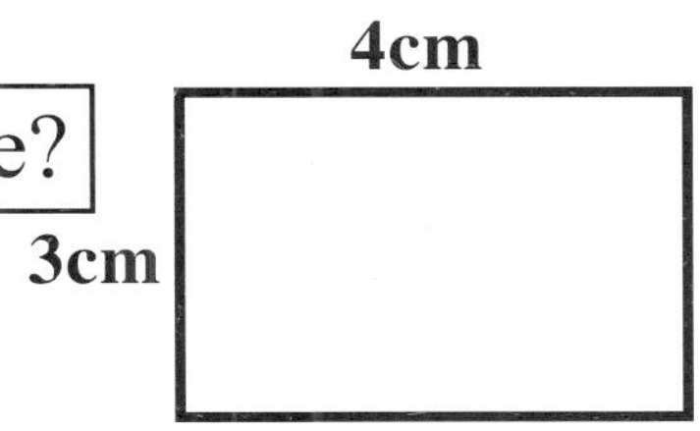

Length + Width + Length + Width

4 + 3 + 4 + 3 = 14cm

Exercise 16: 1a Answer the following:

What are the Perimeters of these Shapes?

1)

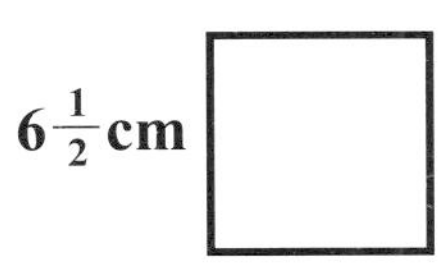

.... cm.

2)

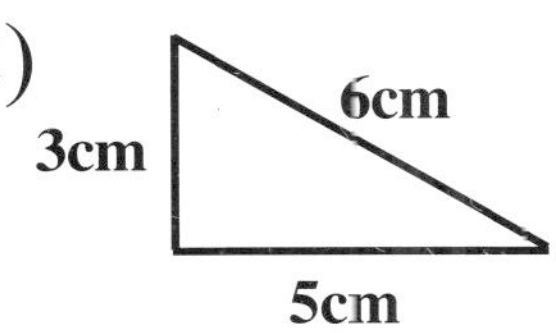

.... cm.

3)

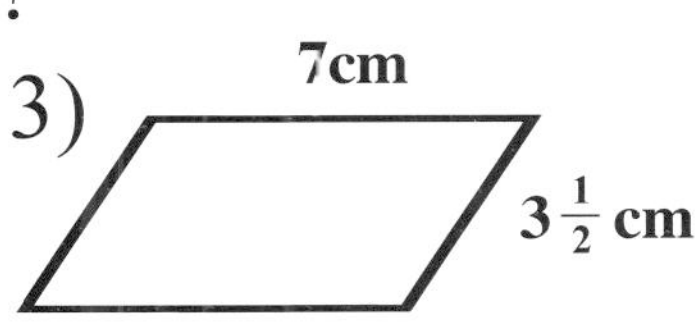

.... cm.

More complex Shapes sometimes have a number of **Missing Measurements** that have to be Calculated.

Example: What is the Perimeter of this Shape?

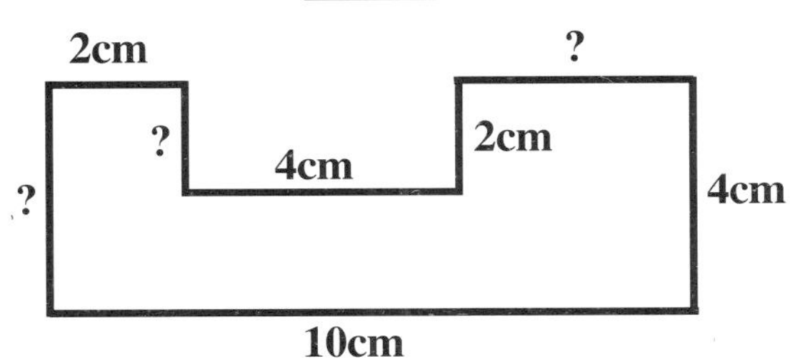

1. Calculate the missing Measurements by working from those given. e.g. If the Length is 10cm, the missing amount at the top must be 10 − (2 + 4) = **4cm.**

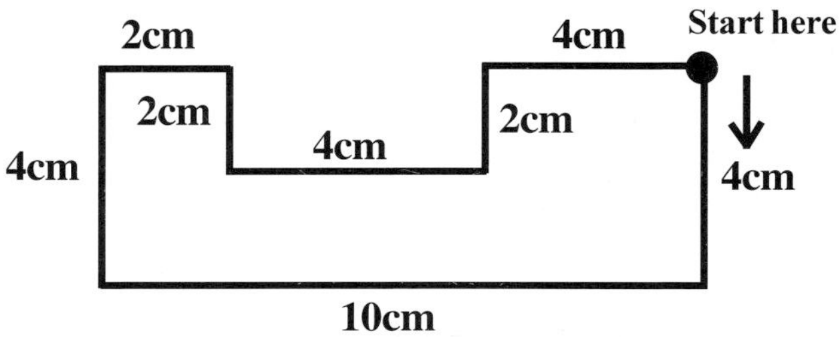

2. Mark your starting point to avoid counting twice.
3. Add up all the Sides.
   4 + 10 + 4 + 2 + 2 + 4 + 2 + 4
   The Perimeter = 32cm.

Exercise 16: 1b Write the Perimeter in the centre of each object:

4)
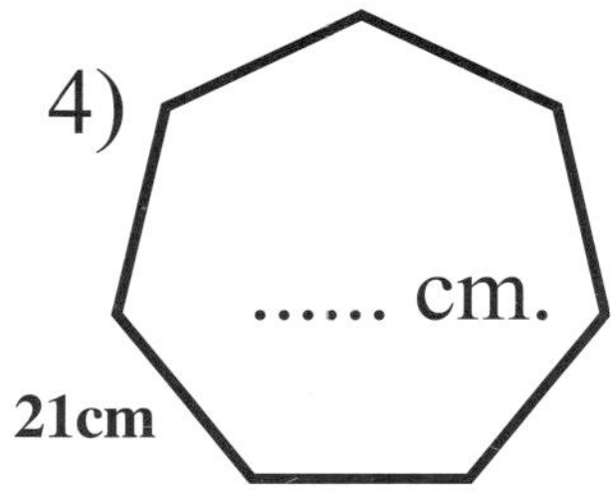

5)
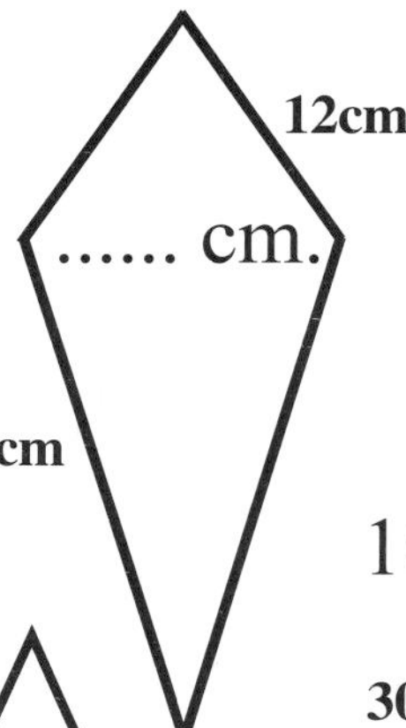

6)
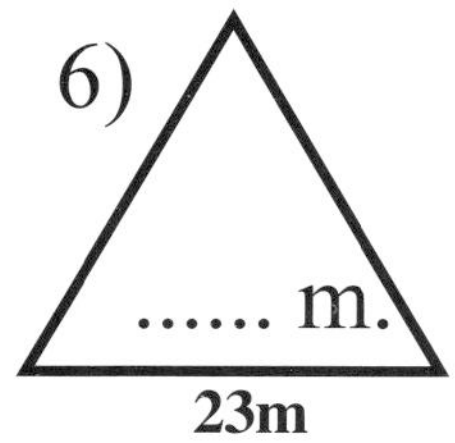

7)
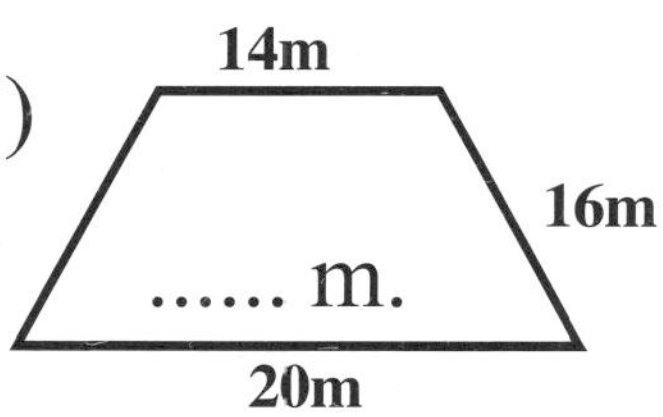

8)
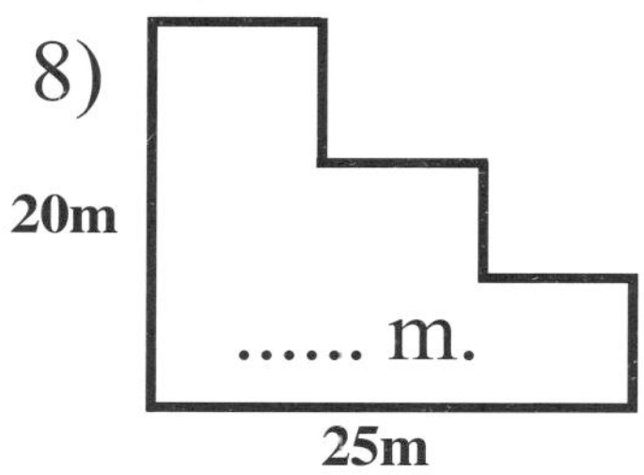

9)
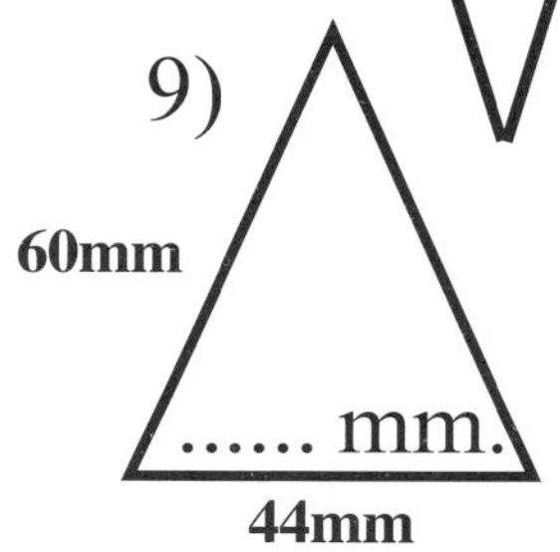

10)
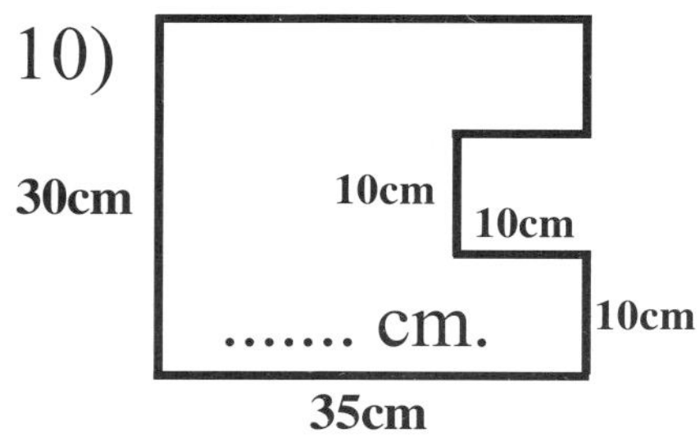

Score Out of Ten →

2. Area

a. Squares and Rectangles

Area of a Square or Rectangle = Length × Width

Example: Area of a Rectangle measuring **4cm** by **3cm.**

Area = 4cm × 3cm = 12cm^2

4 lots of 3 Squares make 12 Squares (Area is written as 'Squared').

Exercise 16: 2a Calculate the Area of the following:

1) What is the Area of a Rectangle that measures **7 metres** in Length and **5 metres** in Width? .... m^2.

2) The Area of this Rectangle is: (each Square is **1cm** in length) .... cm^2.

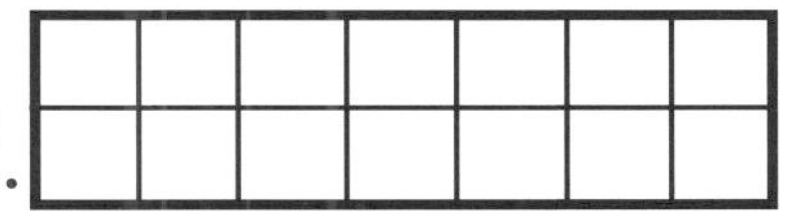

Learn as an **Aid to Memory**.

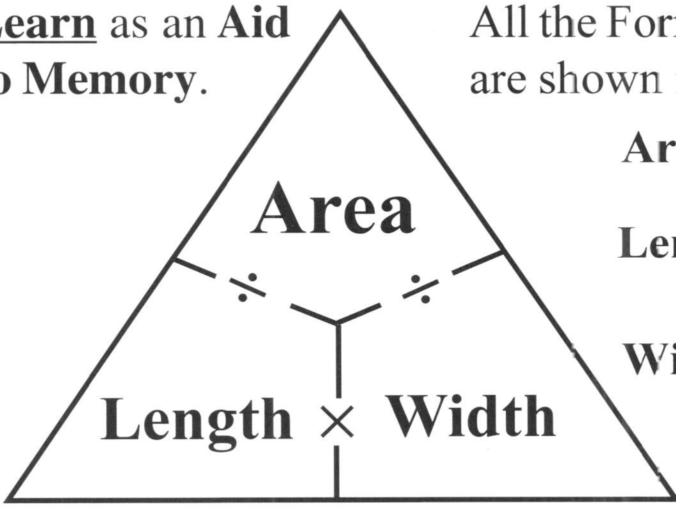

All the Formulae for Rectangles are shown in the Formula Triangle.

Area = Length × Width

$$\textbf{Length} = \frac{\textbf{Area}}{\textbf{Width}}$$

$$\textbf{Width} = \frac{\textbf{Area}}{\textbf{Length}}$$

(See **Book 4** for **Formula Triangles**)

Finding the **Length** or **Width** of a Rectangle:

Length = Area ÷ Width | **Width = Area ÷ Length**

Example: The Area of a Rectangle is **$12cm^2$** and its Width is **3cm**. What is its Length?

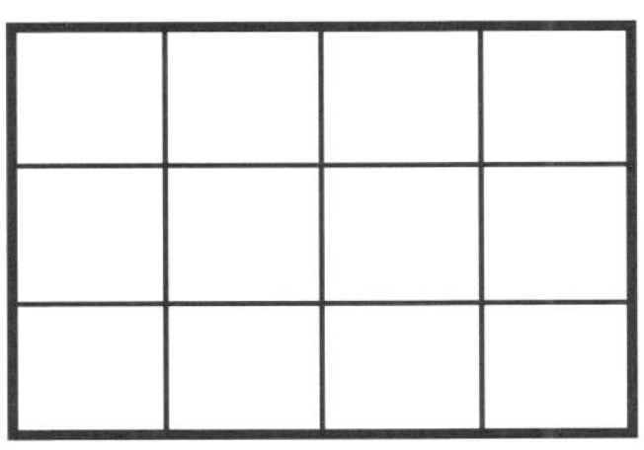

Length = Area ÷ Width

$$\textbf{Length} = \frac{\textbf{Area}}{\textbf{Width}} = \frac{\textbf{12}}{\textbf{3}}$$

The Length of the Rectangle = 4cm.

Exercise 16: 2b Calculate the following:

3) What is the Length of a Rectangle that has an Area of **$30cm^2$** and a Width of **5cm**? .... cm.

4) If a Rectangle measures **10m** in Length and its Area is **60m²**, what is its Width? .... m.

5) A Square has an Area of **49cm²**. What does each of its Sides measure? .... cm.

Some questions link **Perimeter and Area**:

Example 1:

The Perimeter of a Square is **20cm**. Find the Area.

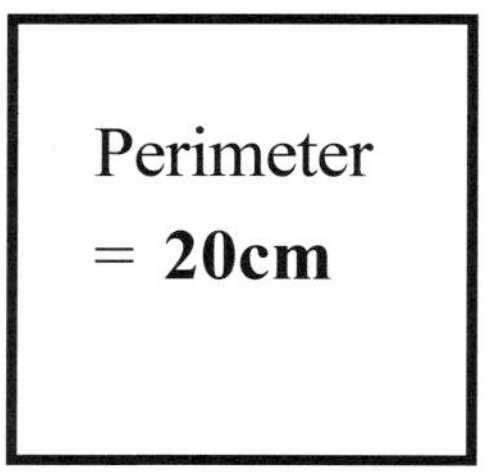

Find the Length of each Side

Side = **20** ÷ **4** = **5cm**

Find the Area

Area = Length × Width

Area = **5** × **5** = **25cm²**.

Example 2:

A Rectangle has a Perimeter of **18cm** and the Length is **5cm**. Find the Area.

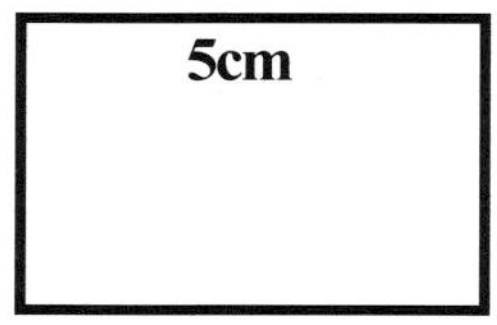

Perimeter = L + W + L + W

= **5** + W + **5** + W

= **10** + W + W

Missing Widths **18 – 10** = **8**

Divide **8** ÷ **2** = **4cm**

Area = **5** × **4** = **20cm²**.

Exercise 16: 2c Calculate the following:

6) The Area of a Square is **36m²**. The Perimeter would measure .... m.

7) If the Perimeter of a Rectangle is **17cm** and the Width is **2.5cm**, what would the Area be? .... cm².

8) a) The Length of this Rectangle would be .... m.

b) The Perimeter would measure .... m.

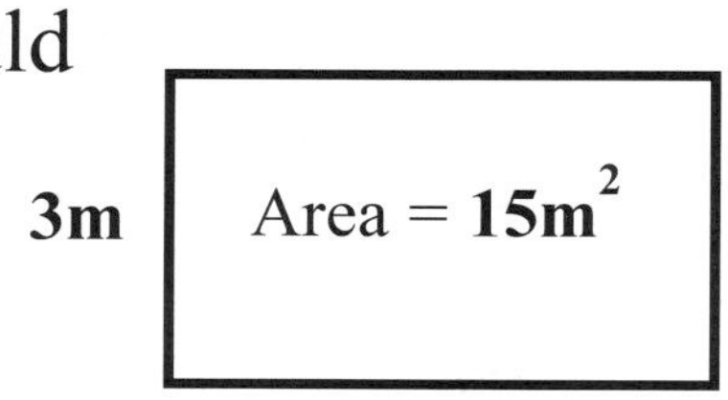

Complex Shapes have to be Divided up to Calculate Area.

What is the Area of this Shape?

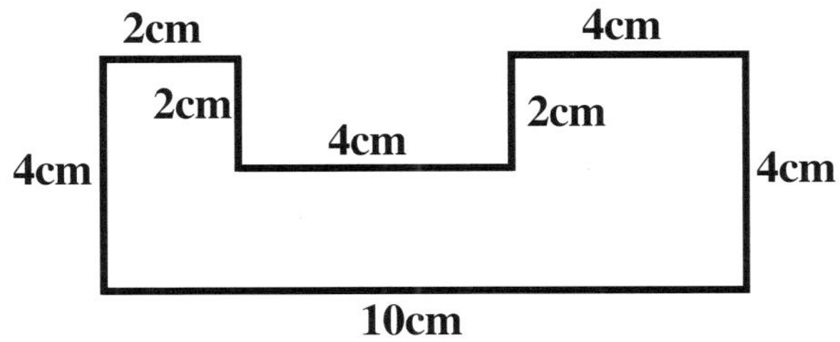

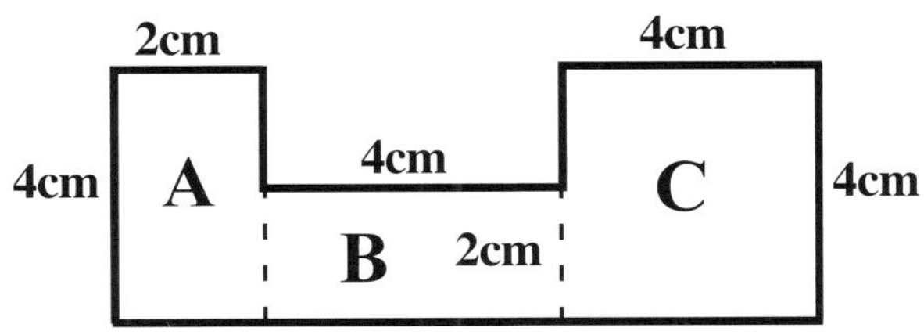

1. Divide up the Shape.
2. Work out each Area.
   Area **A** is $2 \times 4 = \mathbf{8cm^2}$
   Area **B** is $2 \times 4 = \mathbf{8cm^2}$
   Area **C** is $4 \times 4 = \mathbf{16cm^2}$
3. **Add** Areas A, B and C together for the Total Area.
   $8 + 8 + 16 = \mathbf{32cm^2}$.

The Area is 32cm².

Exercise 16: 2d

Calculate the following:

Score

9) The Area of the shaded border is .... cm^2.

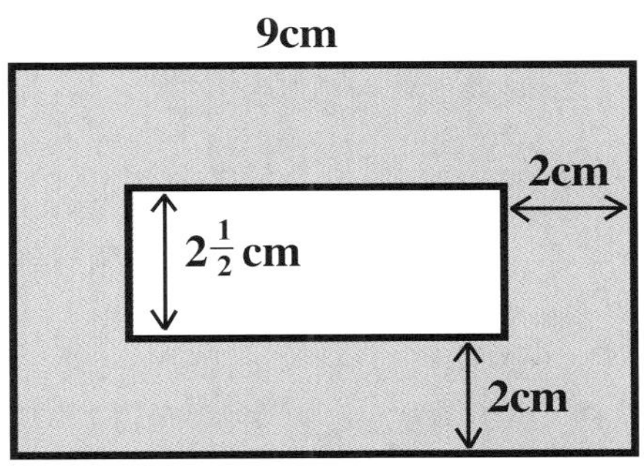

10)

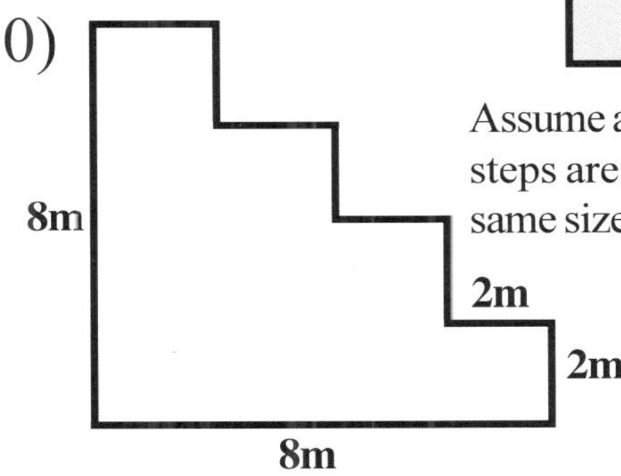

Assume all the steps are the same size.

The Area of this Shape is .... m^2

b. Triangles

Two Triangles of equal size can be fitted into a Rectangle.
Therefore the Area of a Triangle is half that of a Rectangle.

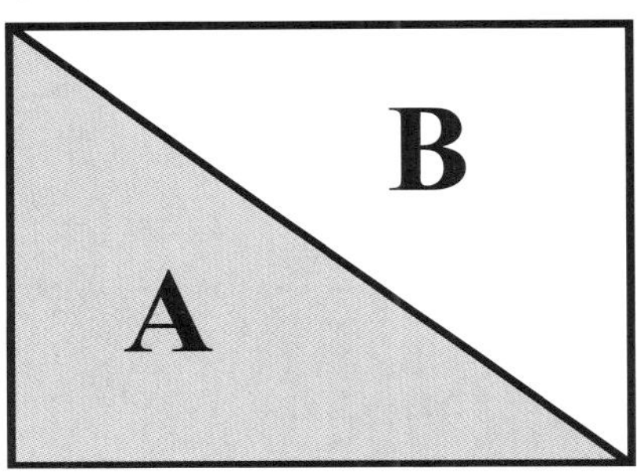

or

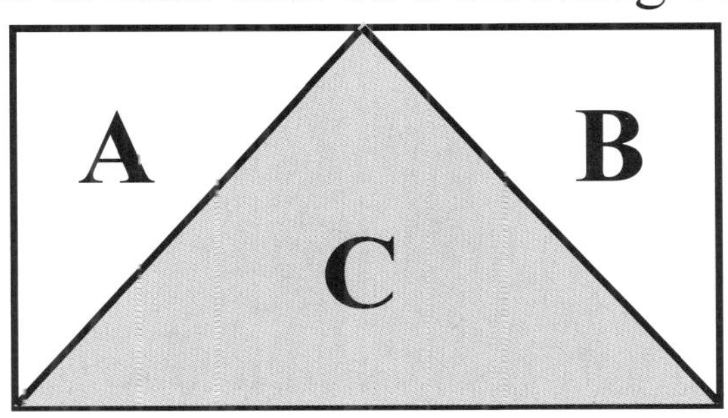

Area A = Area B

Area A + Area B = Area C

Learn as an **Aid to Memory**.

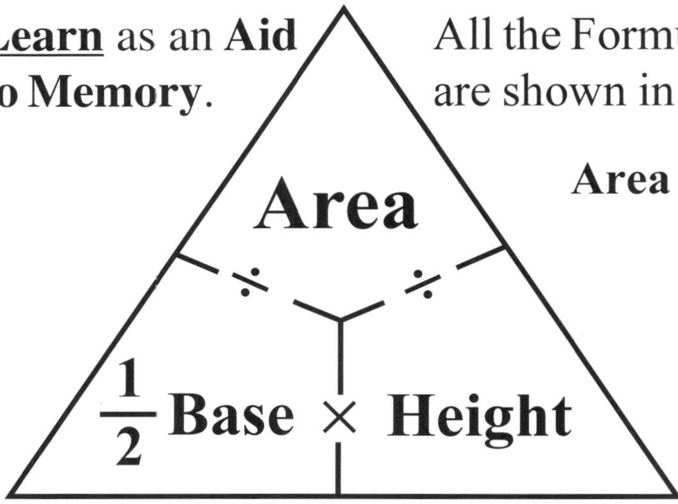

All the Formulae for Triangles are shown in the Formula Triangle.

$$\textbf{Area} = \tfrac{1}{2}\,\textbf{Base} \times \textbf{Height}$$

$$\tfrac{1}{2}\,\textbf{Base} = \frac{\textbf{Area}}{\textbf{Height}}$$

$$\textbf{Height} = \frac{\textbf{Area}}{\tfrac{1}{2}\,\textbf{Base}}$$

The Formulae can be converted to:
$$A = \frac{B \times H}{2} \qquad B = \frac{2 \times A}{H} \qquad H = \frac{2 \times A}{B}$$

Finding the **Area**:

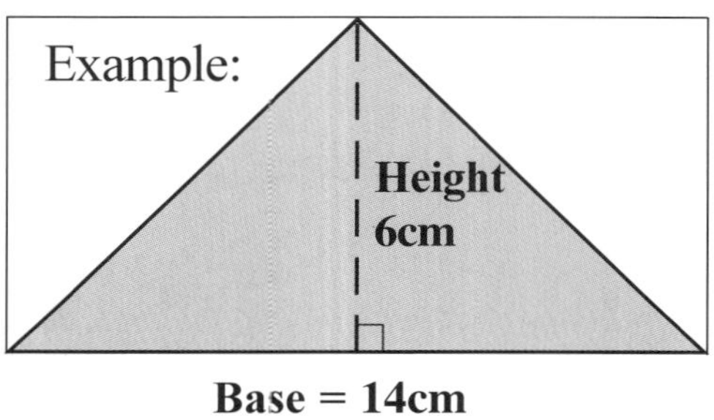

The Area of the Rectangle is:
Area = Length × Width
Halve it for the Triangle Area:

$$\textbf{Area} = \tfrac{1}{2}\,\textbf{Base} \times \textbf{Height}$$
$$= (14 \times 6) \div 2$$
$$= 84 \div 2$$

Area of the Triangle = **42cm^2**

Exercise 16: 3a Calculate the following:

1) Find the Area of this Triangle.

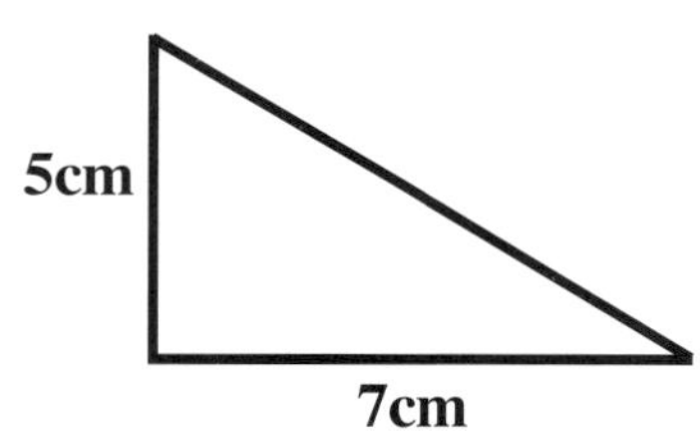

Area = $\frac{1}{2}$ Base × Height
Area = ... cm^2.

2) What is the Area of a Triangle with a Base of **15cm** and a Height of **10cm** .... cm^2.

3) The Base of a Triangle is **8m** and the Height is **3m**. What is the Area? .... m^2.

Finding the **Height**:

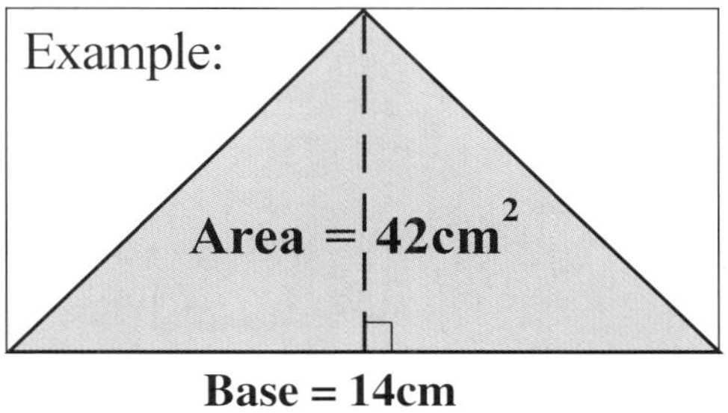

$$\textbf{Height} = \frac{\textbf{Area}}{\frac{1}{2}\textbf{Base}}$$

$$= 42 \div (14 \div 2)$$

$$= 42 \div 7 \text{ or } \frac{42}{7}$$

Height of the Triangle = 6cm

Remember: The standard Formulae can also be used.
$$H = \frac{2 \times A}{B} \qquad H = \frac{2 \times 42}{14} = 6\text{cm}$$

Exercise 16: 3b Calculate the following:

4) A Triangle has a Base of **30mm** and an Area of **360mm²**. What is the Height of the Triangle? .... mm.

5) 

If the Area of this Triangle is **7.2m²**, what would the Height be? .... m.

6) If the Area of a Triangle is **16.5cm²** and the Base is **11cm**, what will the Height measure? .... cm.

Finding the **Base**:

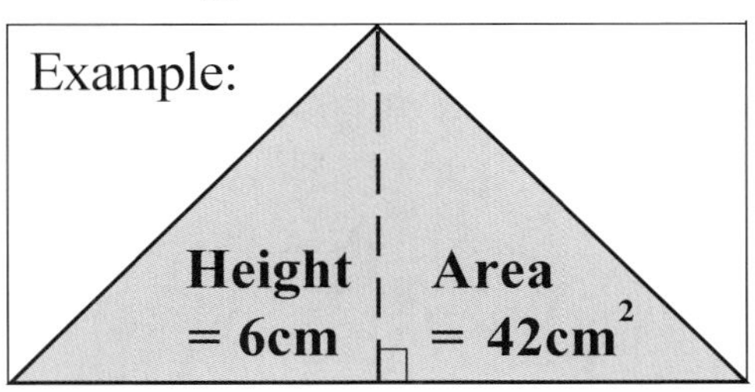

$$\tfrac{1}{2}\textbf{ Base} = \frac{\textbf{Area}}{\textbf{Height}}$$

$$= 42 \div 6$$

$$\tfrac{1}{2}\textbf{ Base} = 7$$

Multiply by 2

$$\textbf{Base} = 7 \times 2$$

The Base of the Triangle = 14cm

Remember: The standard Formulae can also be used.
$$B = \frac{2 \times A}{H} \qquad B = \frac{2 \times 42}{6} = 14\text{cm}$$

Exercise 16: 3c Calculate the following:

Score

7) If the Height of a Triangle is **18cm** and the Area is **243cm²**, what will the Base be? .... cm.

8)

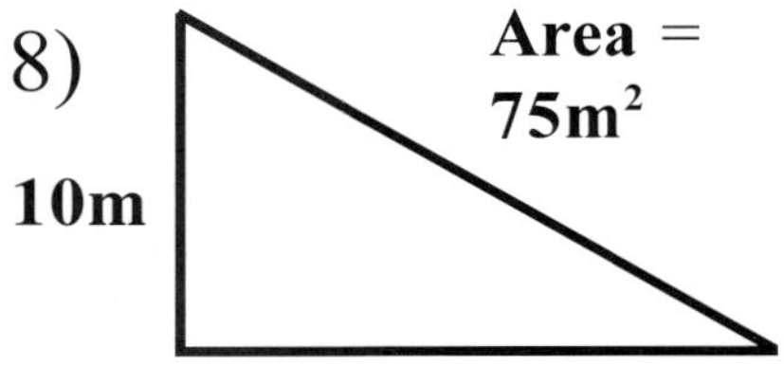

The Base measures .... m.

9)

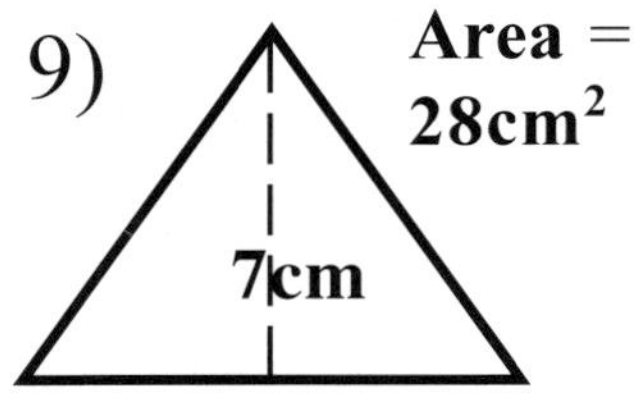

The Base will be .... cm.

10) Fill in the missing Measurements on this table.

Base	Height	Area
20mm	**25mm**	a) .... mm^2
b) .... cm	**9cm**	**63cm²**
c) .... m	**12m**	**60m²**

c. Parallelograms & Rhombuses (Rhombi)

The Area of a Triangle is **A** = $\frac{1}{2}$ **B** × **H**

A Parallelogram is two Equal Triangles, Formula: **A** = **B** × **H**

They split into two Equal Triangles.

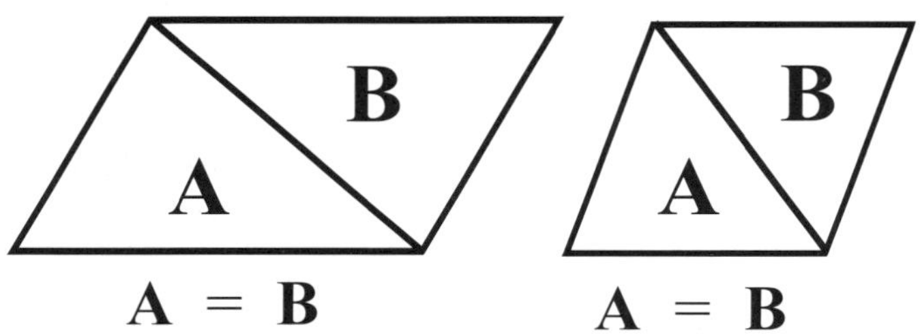

Learn as an **Aid to Memory**.

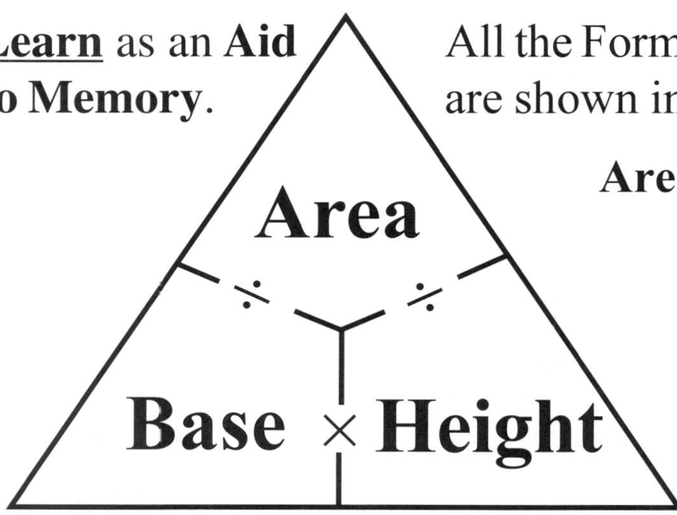

All the Formulae for Parallelograms are shown in the Formula Triangle.

Area = **Base × Height**

Height = $\frac{\textbf{Area}}{\textbf{Base}}$

Base = $\frac{\textbf{Area}}{\textbf{Height}}$

Finding the Area, Base and Height of a Parallelogram:

Example:

Area of the Parallelogram.

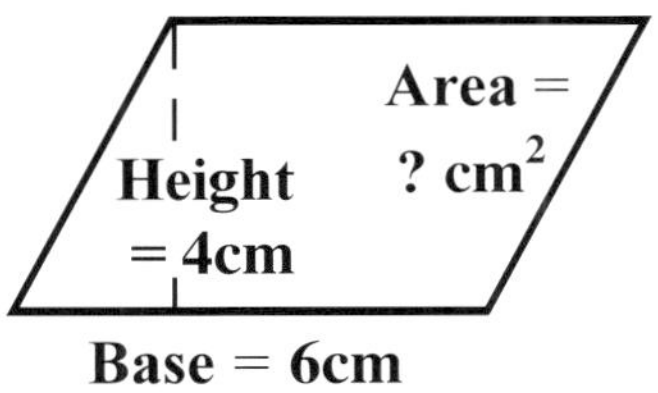

$$\textbf{Area} = B \times H$$
$$= 6 \times 4$$
$$= 24cm^2$$

Example:

Base of the Parallelogram.

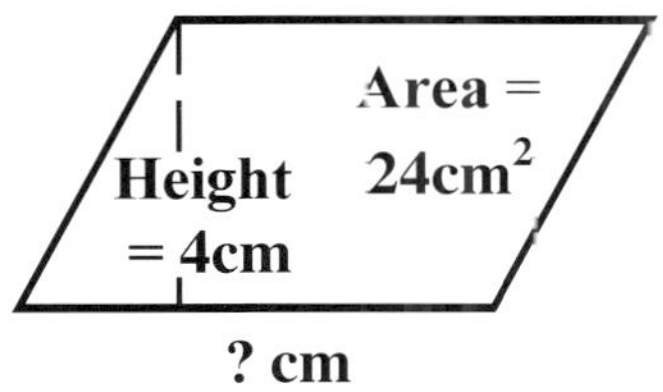

$$\textbf{Base} = A \div H$$
$$= 24 \div 4$$
$$= 6cm$$

Example:

Height of the Parallelogram.

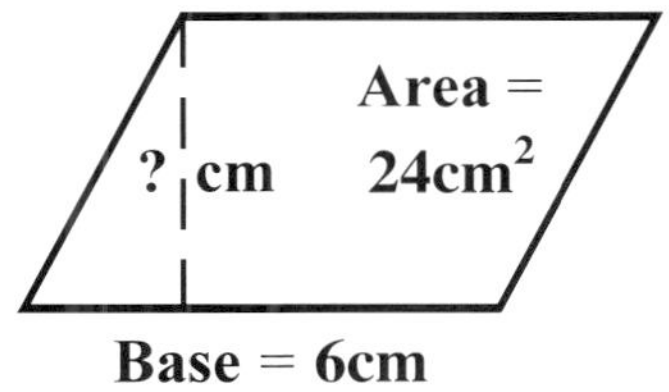

$$\textbf{Height} = A \div B$$
$$= 24 \div 6$$
$$= 4cm$$

Exercise 16: 4a Calculate the following:

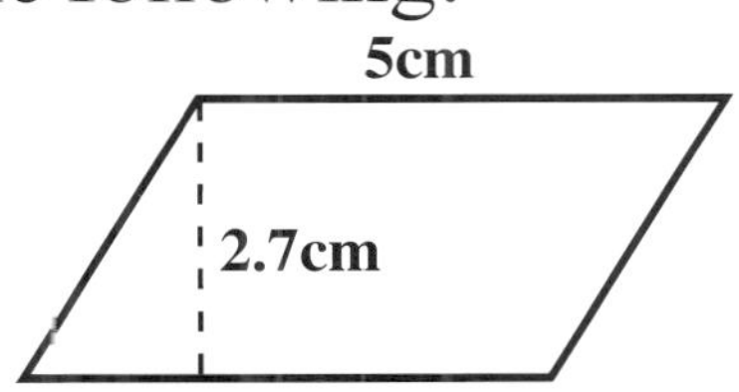

1) What is the Area of this Parallelogram? .... cm^2.

2) If the Base of a Parallelogram is **10cm** and Area is **50cm**, what will the Height be? .... cm.

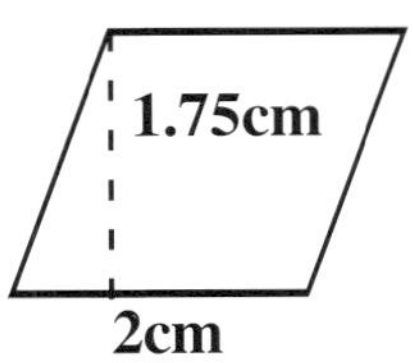

3) What is the Area of this Rhombus? .... cm^2.

4) A Parallelogram has an Area of **15mm²** and its Height is **5mm**. What is the Length of the Base? .... mm.

5) Fill in the missing Measurements on this table for these Parallelograms.

Base	Height	Area
10mm	**15mm**	a) .... mm^2
b) .... cm	**4cm**	**48cm²**
3.5m	c) .... m	**17.5m²**

d. Trapezia (Trapeziums)

Learn as an **Aid to Memory**.

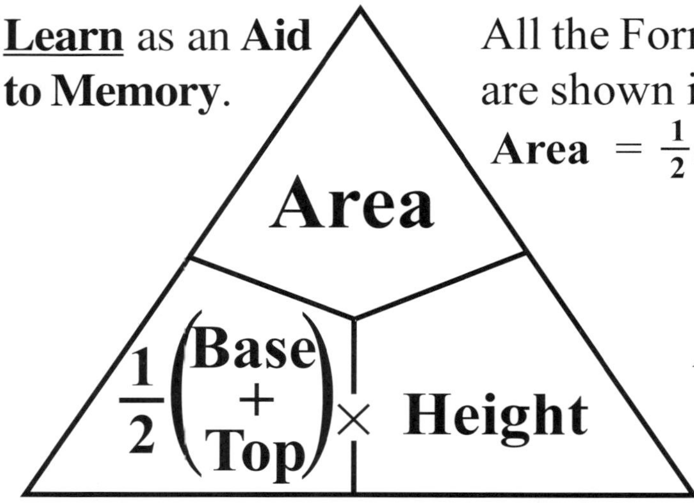

All the Formulae for Trapeziums are shown in the Formula Triangle.

$$\textbf{Area} = \tfrac{1}{2}(\textbf{Base} + \textbf{Top}) \times \textbf{Height}$$

The Formula can be written in this way.

$$A = \frac{(B + T) \times H}{2}$$

The other Formulae are used less often but are shown below.

Finding the **Area**:

Example:

$$\textbf{Area} = \tfrac{1}{2}(\textbf{Base} + \textbf{Top}) \times \textbf{Height}$$

The Area of the Trapezium:

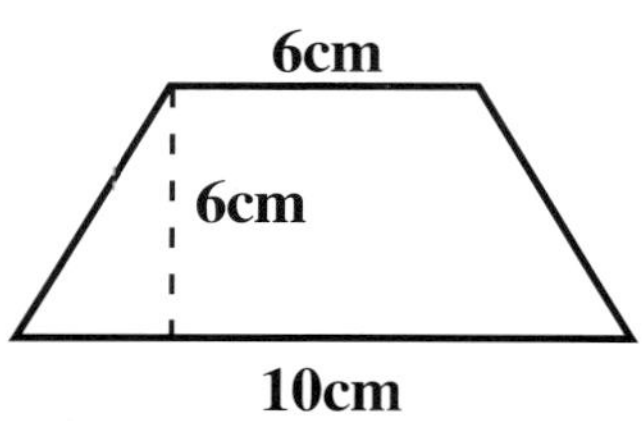

$$= \tfrac{1}{2}(10 + 6) \times 6$$

$$= \tfrac{1}{2} \times 16 \times 6$$

$$= 8 \times 6$$

The Area of the Trapezium $= \mathbf{48cm^2}$

Finding the **Base** or **Top**:

Example:

The top of the Trapezium:

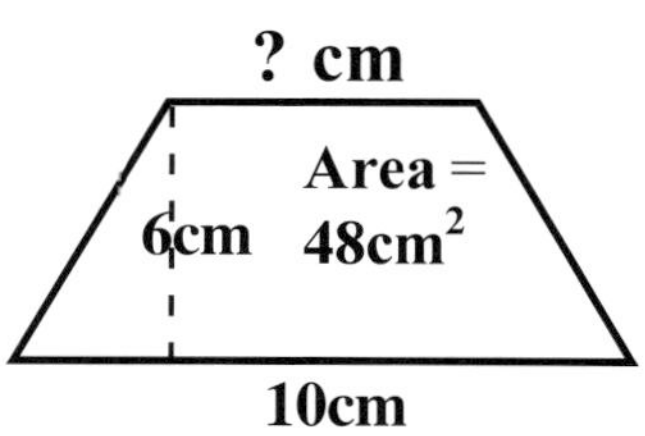

$$\tfrac{1}{2}\begin{pmatrix}\textbf{Base}\\ \textbf{+ Top}\end{pmatrix} = \frac{48}{6}$$

$$\tfrac{1}{2}\begin{pmatrix}\textbf{Base}\\ \textbf{+ Top}\end{pmatrix} = 8$$

Multiply by 2

Base + Top = **16**

Top = **16 − Base**

= **16 − 10**

The Top of the Trapezium = **6cm**

$$\tfrac{1}{2}\begin{pmatrix}\textbf{Base}\\ \textbf{+ Top}\end{pmatrix} = \frac{\textbf{Area}}{\textbf{Height}}$$

Finding the **Height**:
Example:
The Height of the Trapezium:

$$\textbf{Height} = \frac{\textbf{Area}}{\frac{1}{2}(\textbf{Base} + \textbf{Top})}$$

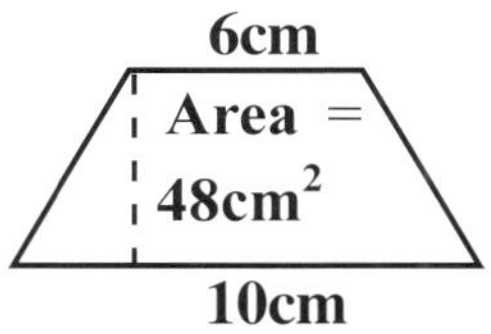

$$= \frac{\textbf{48cm}}{\frac{1}{2}(\textbf{10} + \textbf{6})} = \frac{\textbf{48}}{\textbf{8}}$$

The Height of the Trapezium = **6cm**.

Exercise 16: 4b Calculate the following:

Score

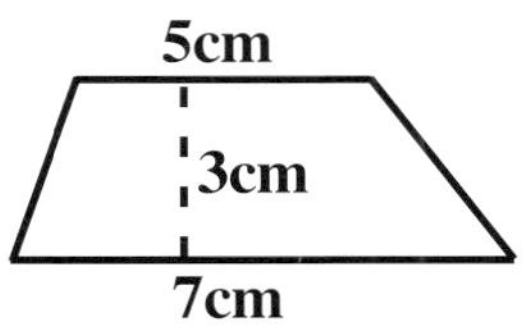

6) Find the Area of this Trapezium? .... cm^2.

7) The Area of a Trapezium is $\mathbf{40cm^2}$. If the Base is **12cm** and the Top is **8cm**, what is the Height? .... cm.

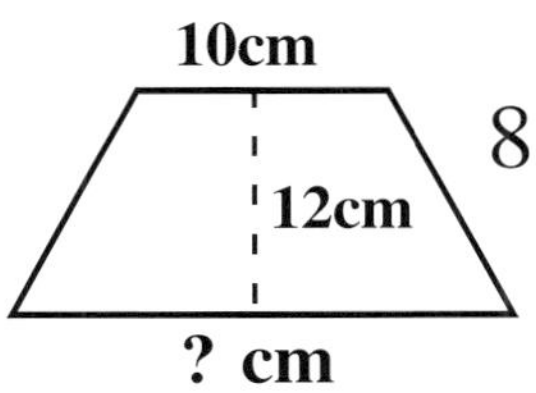

8) The Area of this Trapezium is $\mathbf{144cm^2}$. The Base Length would be .... cm.

9) If the Base of a Trapezium is **15cm**, its Top is **10cm** and its Area is $\mathbf{62.5cm^2}$, its Height will be? .... cm.

10) What would the Length of the Top of this Trapezium be? .... cm.

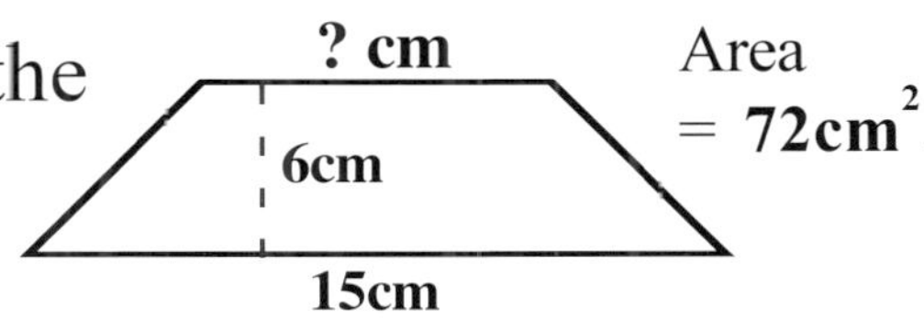

e. Circles

There are two Formulae for Circles:

$$\textbf{Area} = \pi \times \mathbf{r^2}$$

Area = π (3.14) × Radius Squared.

$$\textbf{Circumference} = \pi \times \textbf{D}$$

Circumference = π (3.14) × Diameter

The Greek Symbol π

π or 'pi' = $\dfrac{\text{Circumference}}{\text{Diameter}}$

Its value is **approximately 3** (just over 3). It is usually written as **3.14**.

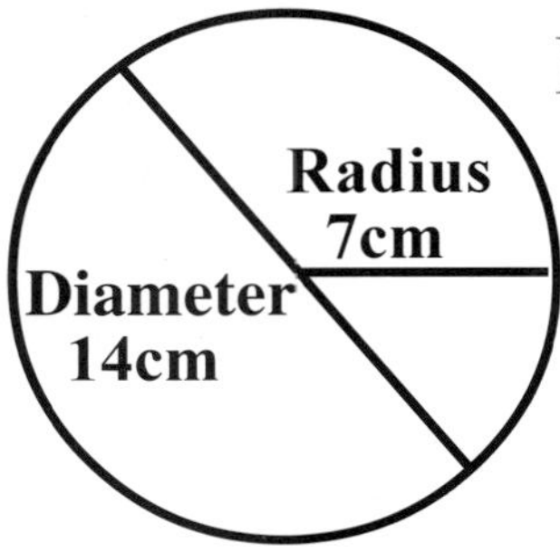

Example: **Find the Area of a Circle with a Radius of 7cm.**

π (**3.14**) can be written as $\approx \frac{22}{7}$

Hence Decimals or Fractions can be used:

Using **Decimals**:

$$\textbf{Area} = \pi \times r^2$$
$$= 3.14 \times 7^2$$
$$= 3.14 \times 49$$
$$= 153.86\text{cm}^2 \text{ or } 154\text{cm}^2 \text{ (rounded)}$$

Using **Fractions**:

$$\textbf{Area} = \pi \times r^2$$
$$= \frac{22}{7} \times 7^2$$
$$= \frac{22}{{}_1\cancel{7}} \times \frac{\cancel{49}^{\,7}}{1}$$
$$= 22 \times 7$$
$$= 154\text{cm}^2$$

Exercise 16: 5a Calculate the following:

Solve the following questions using **Decimals**:

1) If the Radius of a Circle is **4cm**, what is the Area of the circle? .... cm^2.

2) The Diameter of a Circle is **6cm**, so the Area will be .... cm^2.

3) What is the Area of this Semi-circle? .... cm^2.

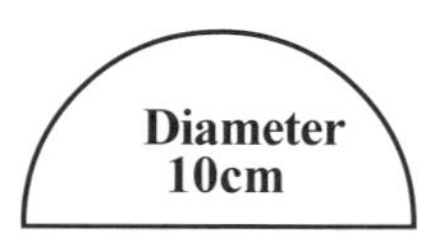

(Halve the answer to find the Area of a Semi-circle e.g. halve the answer to $\pi \times r^2 = \frac{1}{2}\pi r^2$)

Solve the following questions using **Fractions**:

4) The Area of this Circle is .... mm^2.

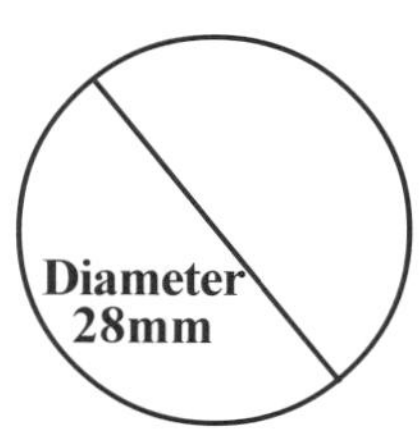

5) The Area of this Circle is .... m^2.

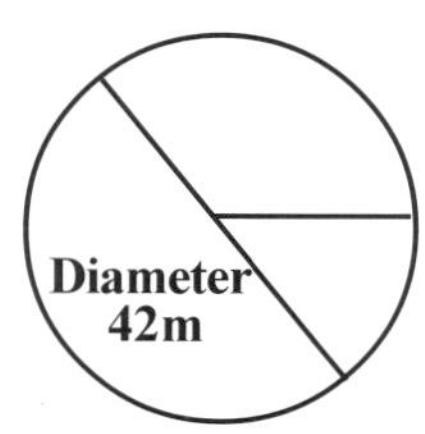

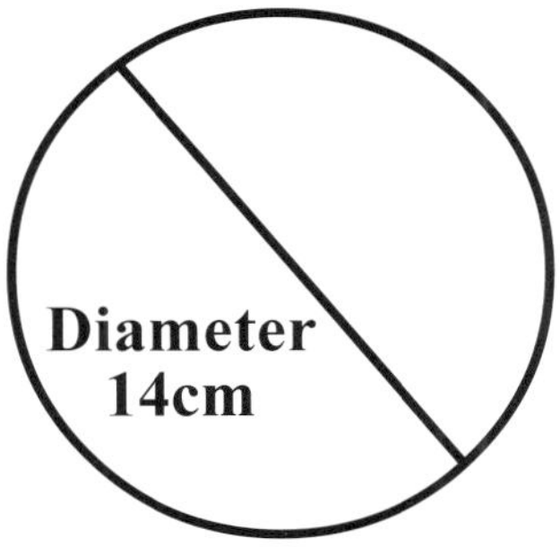

Example: **Find the Circumference of a Circle with a Diameter of 14cm.**

This can be solved in two ways as before using Decimals or Fractions:

Using **Decimals**:

Circumference $= \pi \times \mathbf{D}$

$= \mathbf{3.14 \times 14}$

$=$ **43.96cm or 44cm (rounded)**

Using **Fractions**:

Circumference $= \pi \times \mathbf{D}$

$= \mathbf{\frac{22}{7} \times 14}$

$= \mathbf{\frac{22}{\cancel{7}_{1}} \times \frac{\cancel{14}^{2}}{1}}$

$= \mathbf{22 \times 2}$

$=$ **44cm**

Exercise 16: 5b Calculate the following:

Score

Solve the following questions using **<u>Decimals</u>**:

6) If the Radius of a Circle is **4cm**, the Circumference will be? .... cm.

7) The Diameter of a Circle is **6cm**, so the Circumference will be .... cm.

8) What is the Length of the Arc of this Semi-circle? .... cm.

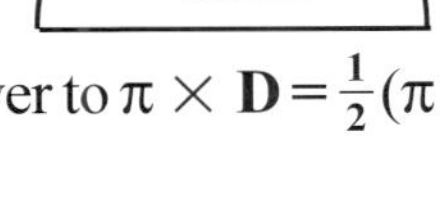

(Halve the Circumference to find the Arc of a Semi-circle e.g. halve the answer to $\pi \times \mathbf{D} = \frac{1}{2}(\pi \times \mathbf{D})$)

Work out the Circumference using **<u>Fractions</u>**:

9) .... mm.

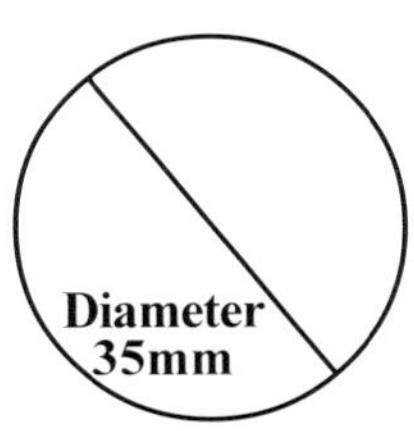

10) .... m.

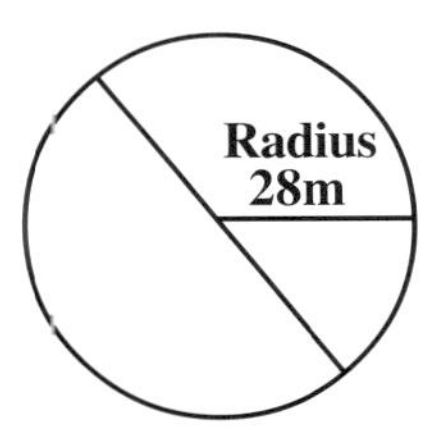

f. Annuli (Singular Annulus)

An Annulus is a ring formed by two Concentric Circles.

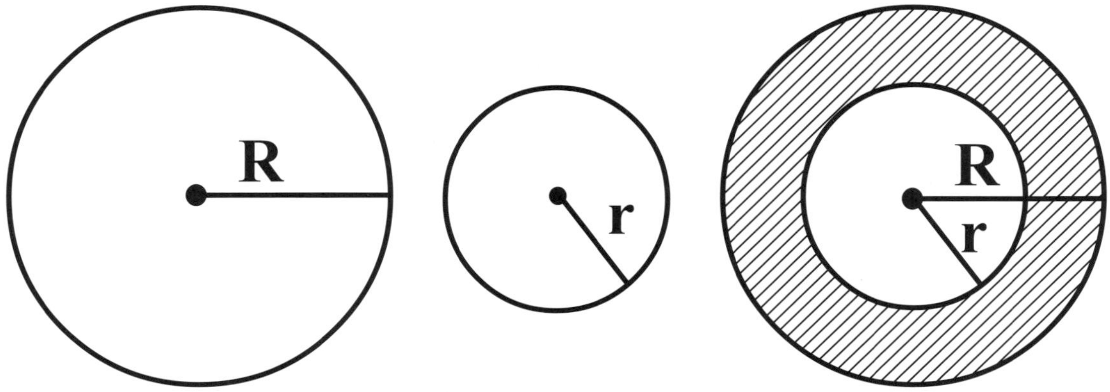

The Radius of the **larger circle** is **R**. The Radius of the **smaller circle** is **r**. The shaded part is the **Annulus**.

Annulus Area = Large Circle Area − Small Circle Area.

The Formula is as follows: $\textbf{Area} = \pi R^2 - \pi r^2$

It can also be written as: $\textbf{Area} = \pi(R^2 - r^2)$

Example:

Find the Area between two Concentric Circles (Annulus) whose Radii are **5cm** and **3cm**.

$$A = \pi(R^2 - r^2) \longrightarrow A = 3.14\,(5^2 - 3^2)$$

$$A = 3.14\,(25 - 9)$$

$$A = 3.14 \times 16$$

Area of the Annulus = 50.24cm². $\left(50.24\,\text{cm}^2\right)$

Exercise 16: 6a Find the Area of the Annulus to 2 d.p.:

1) Outer Radius of **10cm** and Inner Radius of **7cm**.

$A = \pi(R^2 - r^2)$

Do your working here.

$A = 3.14\ (10^2 - 7^2)$

Area of the Annulus is .... cm^2.

2) Outer Radius **13cm**, Inner Radius **5cm** .... cm^2.

3) Outer Radius **15m**, Inner Radius **6m** .... m^2.

4) Outer Radius **1.5cm**, Inner Radius **0.6cm** .... cm^2.

5) Outer Radius **6cm**, Inner Radius **2cm** .... cm^2.

g. Surface Area of a Cuboid

The Total Surface Area of any solid figure is the SUM of the Areas of all its Faces.

Total Surface Area of Cuboid = Sum of Areas of all its Faces.

Example:

What is the Total Surface Area of a Cuboid **8cm** long, **5cm** wide and **3cm** high?

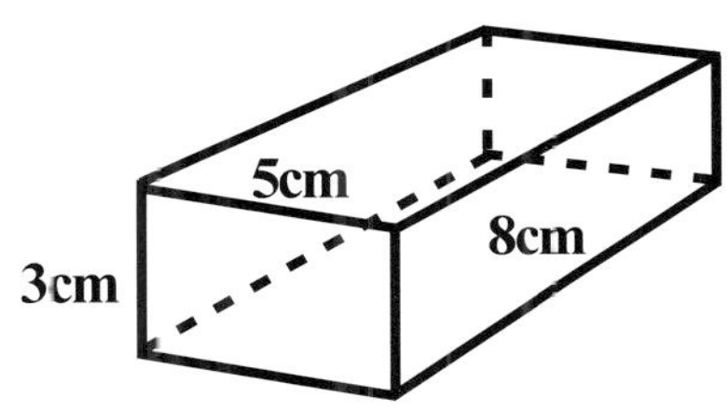

$8 \times 3 = 24$
$8 \times 3 = 24$
$8 \times 5 = 40$
$8 \times 5 = 40$
$3 \times 5 = 15$
$3 \times 5 = 15$
Area = $158cm^2$

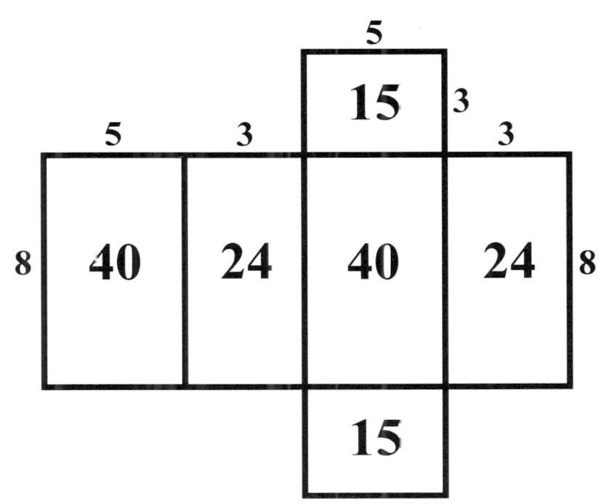

Total Surface Area of Cuboid = $158cm^2$.

Total Surface Area of a **Cube** is **6 Times** the Area of one Face.

Example: Find the Surface Area of a Cube **7cm** long.

Area of one Face $= 7 \times 7 = 49$

Total Surface Area $= 6 \times 49 = 294cm^2$.

Exercise 16: 6b Find the Surface Area:

Score

6)

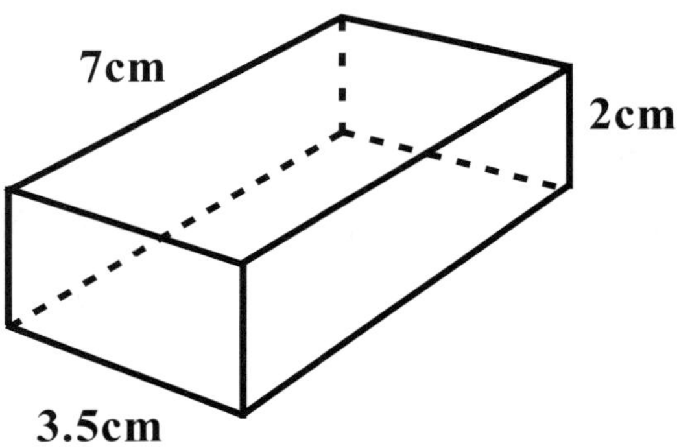

$2 \times 3.5 =$ ....

$2 \times 3.5 =$ ....

$7 \times 3.5 =$ ....

$7 \times 3.5 =$ ....

$7 \times 2 =$ ....

$7 \times 2 =$ ....

Area = ...cm^2

7)

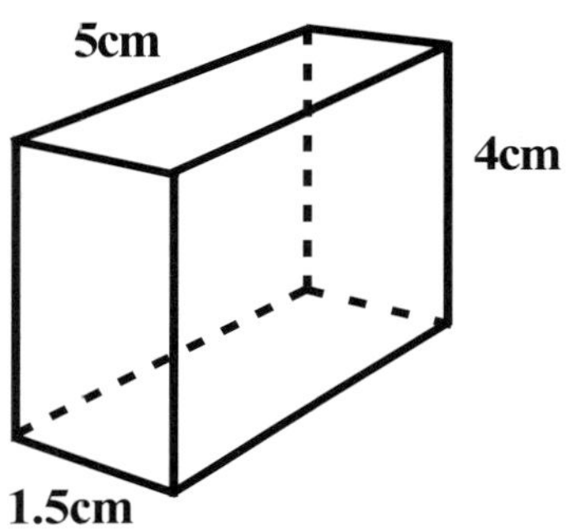

Total Surface Area = ... cm^2.

8)

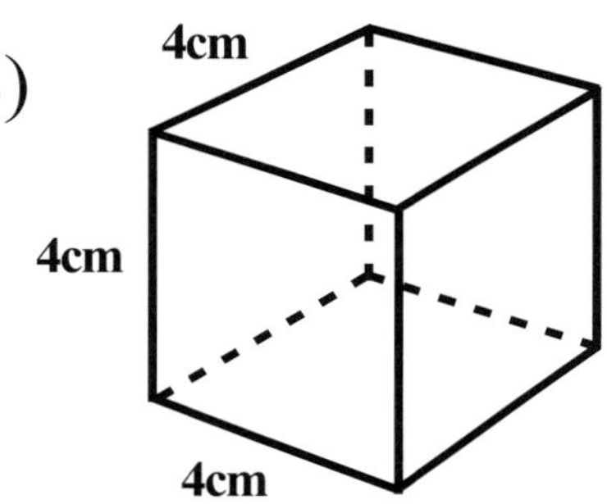

Total Surface Area = ... cm^2.

9) Find the Total Surface area of a Cuboid **35mm** long, **22mm** wide and **50mm** high.

Total Surface Area = ... mm^2.

10) What is the Total Surface Area of a box shaped like a Cube, that is **5m** long?

Total Surface Area = ... m^2.

3. Area and Metric Conversions

Some questions are given in one Metric Measurement but the answer has to be given in another Metric Measurement. This is complicated by the Squaring of Measurements.

Example 1:

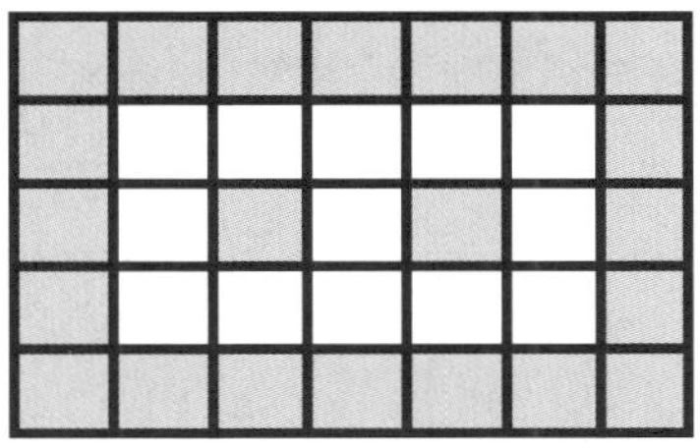

A kitchen is tiled with grey and white tiles each measuring **70cm × 70cm**. What is the Total Area covered by the grey tiles in **Square Metres**?

This question requires an answer in Square Metres but the original measurements given are in Centimetres.

1. **Multiply** Dimensions for the Area of each tile **70cm × 70cm** = **4,900cm^2**
2. **Multiply** by number of tiles for the Total Area **4,900cm^2 × 22** = **107,800cm^2**

Pay special attention to this stage as this is different:

3. **Convert to Metres** - This involves two stages:
   a. Move the Decimal Point **two** places to the left - **Divide by 100**.
   b. Repeat process as the original numbers were Squared - **Divide by 100**.

Stage a. Move the Decimal Point **two** places left. **Stage b.** Move the Decimal Point **two** places left.

107,800cm^2 ⟶ 1,078 ⟶ 10.78m^2

Example 2:

The Area of the small Triangle is **200mm^2**. What is the Area of the large Triangle in Centimetres? .... cm^2

The information is given in Square Millimetres, but the answer is required in Square Centimetres.

1. **Multiply** by **4** to find the Total Area in mm^2 **4 × 200mm^2** = **800mm^2**

2. **Convert to Centimetres** - Again this involves two stages:
   a. Move the Decimal Point **one** place to the left - **Divide by 10**.
   b. Repeat process as the original numbers were Squared - **Divide by 10**.

Stage a. Move the Decimal Point **one** place left. **Stage b.** Move the Decimal Point **one** place left.

800mm^2 ⟶ 80 ⟶ 8cm^2

Note: Conversion from larger to smaller units requires the Decimal Point to be moved to the right.

Example: Convert **$400cm^2$** to **mm^2**. Move the decimal point **2** places to the right. **$40,000mm^2$**

Equivalent Metric Area Conversions:

$100mm^2$ ($10mm \times 10mm$) = **$1cm^2$** (Move decimal point **2** places left).

$10,000cm^2$ ($100cm \times 100cm$) = **$1m^2$** (Move decimal point **4** places left).

$10,000m^2$ ($100m \times 100m$) = **1ha (hectare)** (Move d.p. **4** places left).

100ha ($10ha \times 10ha$) = **$1km^2$** (Move d.p. **2** places left).

Exercise 16: 7 Convert the following:

Score

1) **$4,000cm^2$** to **m^2** .... m^2.
2) **$2km^2$** to **hectares** .... ha.
3) **$500mm^2$** to **cm^2** .... cm^2.
4) **$20m^2$** to **cm^2** .... cm^2.
5) **5ha** to **m^2** .... m^2.
6) **$300mm^2$** to **cm^2** .... cm^2.
7) Find in ha the Area of a Rectangle **320m** long and **100m** wide .... ha. (Multiply then Convert)
8) How many hectares in:
   a) **$5km^2$**? .... ha.
   b) **$7.5km^2$**? .... ha.
9) A garden path is made up of paving slabs measuring **80cm × 80cm.** (Multiply then Convert)
   What is the Total Area covered by the:
   a) grey tiles in **Square Metres**? .... m^2.
   b) white tiles in **Square Metres**? .... m^2.

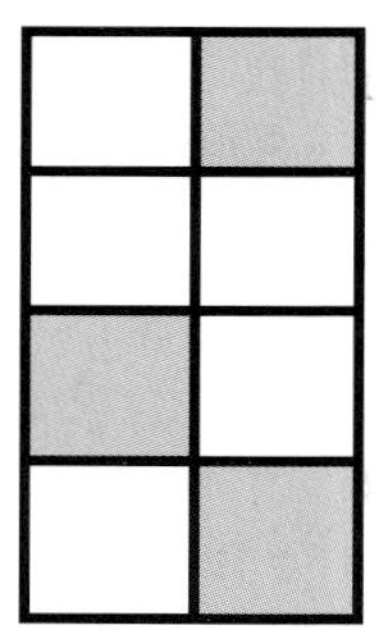

10) The Area of the Hexagon is **$15m^2$**. What is the Area of the shaded Triangle in the Hexagon in square Centimetres?
   .... cm^2 (Convert first then Divide)

4. Volume

a. Prisms

A Prism is a Solid three-dimensional Shape (See **Book 4**).
- Both ends are exactly the same Size and Shape.
- Both ends are Parallel to each other.

The Formula for calculating the Volume of **all** Prisms is the same.

Volume = Area of Base × Length
(Cross-section)

Example:

Find the Volume of a Hexagonal Prism.

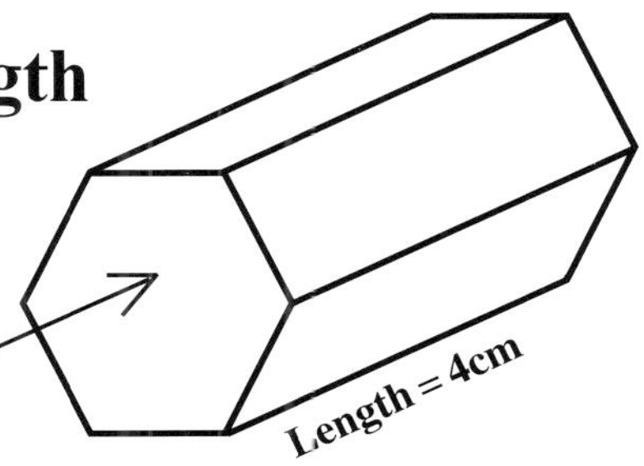

Volume = 25 × 4 = 100cm^3

Exercise 16: 8a Calculate the following:

1) A door wedge is shaped like a trapezium. Work out the Volume of this door wedge.
Remember: Area of a Trapezium is:

$$\text{Area} = \frac{(\text{Base} + \text{Top}) \times \text{Height}}{2}$$

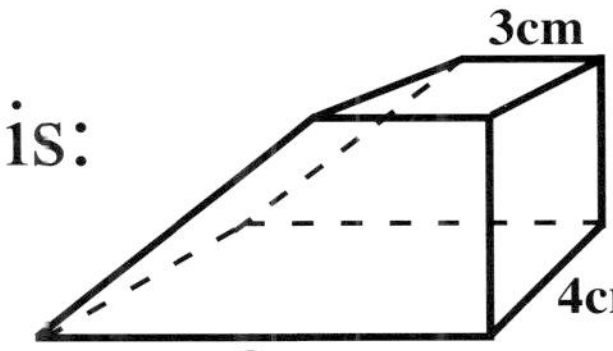

The Volume of the wedge is ....cm^3.

b. Cubes and Cuboids

The Volume of a Cuboid can be worked out by counting the Cubes in a Shape.

Example: | What is the Volume of this Cube? |

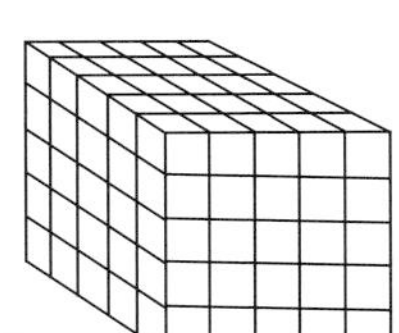

1. **Count** the number of **1cm** Cubes on the front face (25 Cubes).
2. **Multiply** the number by the number of Slices (5 Slices).

Volume = Number of Cubes on front face × Number of Slices.

Volume = 25 × 5 = 125cm^3 (Volume is written as 'Cubed').

Exercise 16: 8b Write the Volume of the following:

2) a) 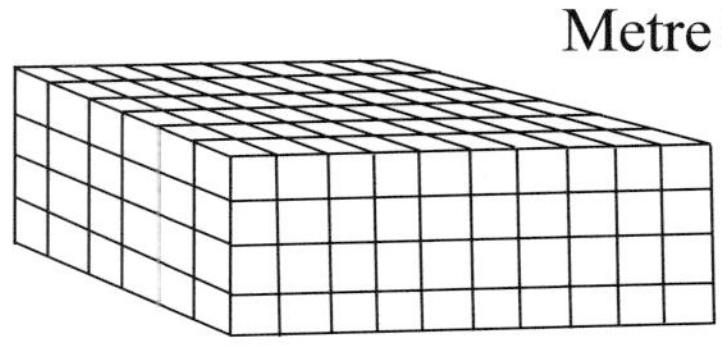

.... m^3.

b) 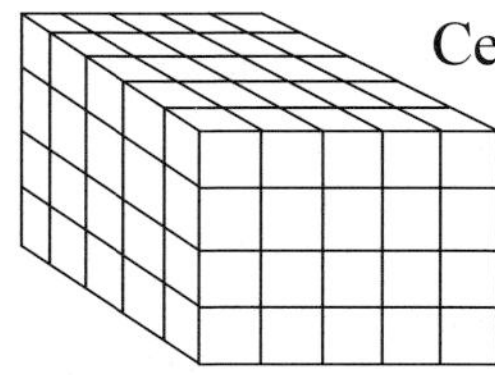

.... cm^3.

Using the Formula:

Volume = Width × Height × Length

This is the same as Area of Cross section × Length.

Example: What is the Volume of this Cube?

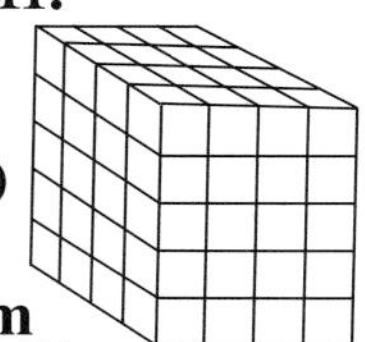

Volume = 4 × 5 × 4 = 80cm³.

Exercise 16: 8c Write the Volume of the following:

3) 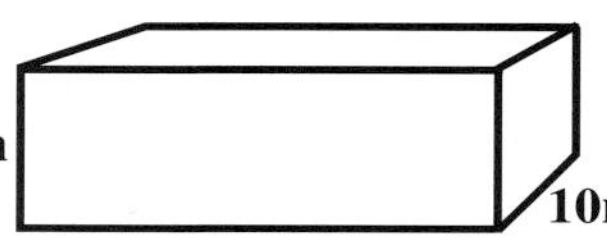

.... mm^3.

4) 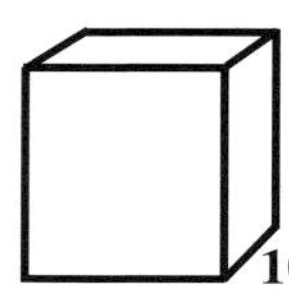

.... cm^3.

Example:

Find the Volume of this shape.

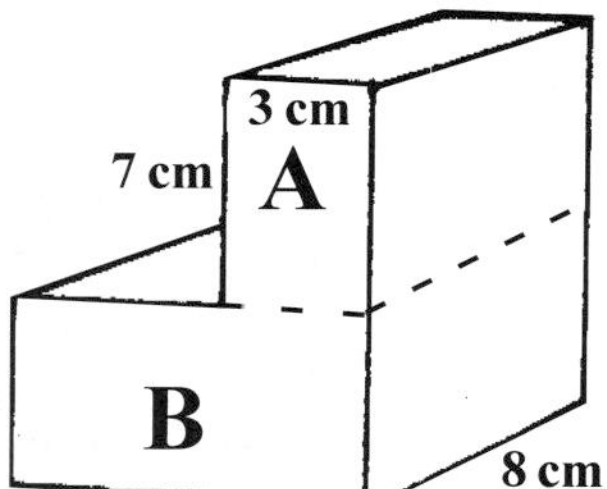

To find the Volume of more complex Shapes they need to be Divided up.

1. Divide the Shape into Cuboids (A and B).
2. Calculate the Volume of each part separately.
3. Add the Volumes for the Total volume.

Shape A = 7 × 3 × 8 = 168cm³

Shape B = 6 × 8 × 8 = 384cm³

Shape A + Shape B = 168cm³ + 384cm³

Total Volume = 552cm³.

This is the same as Area of Cross section × Length

= (7 × 3) + (6 × 8) × Length

= 69 × 8 = **552cm³**

Exercise 16: 8d Find the Volume of the following:

5) a) .... cm^3.

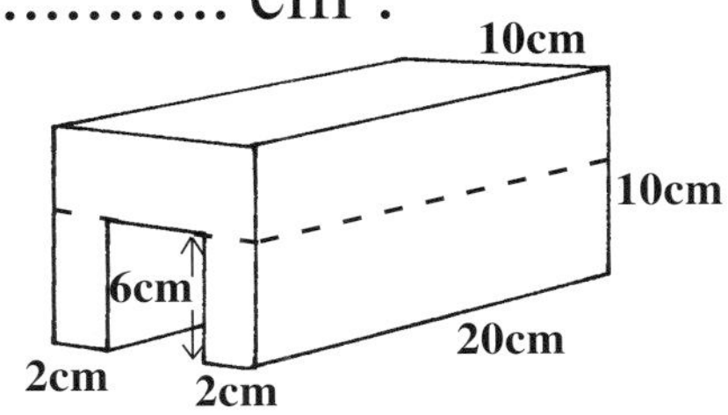

b) .... m^3.

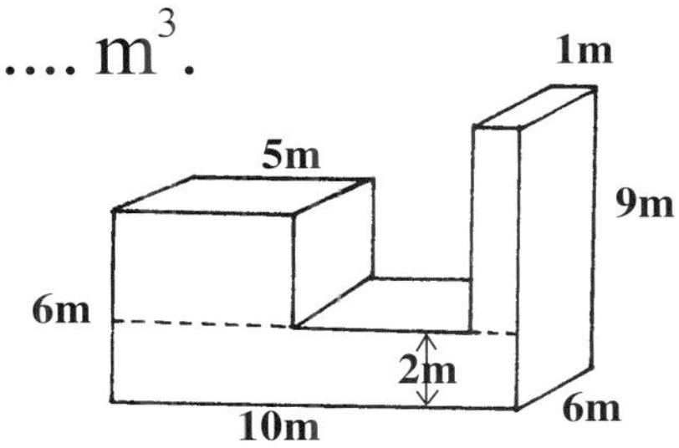

Example: Find the missing Dimension of this Shape.

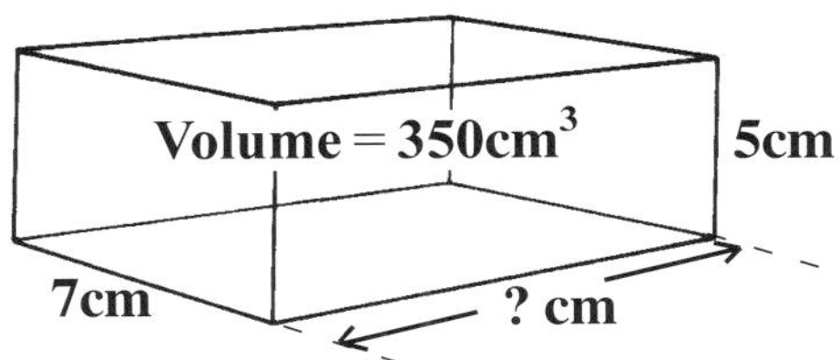

1. **Multiply** the given Dimensions.

$7 \times 5 = 35$

2. **Divide** into the Volume.

$350 \div 35 = 10\text{cm}$

Missing Side = 10cm.

Exercise 16: 8e Write the Length of the missing Side:

6) a)........... m.

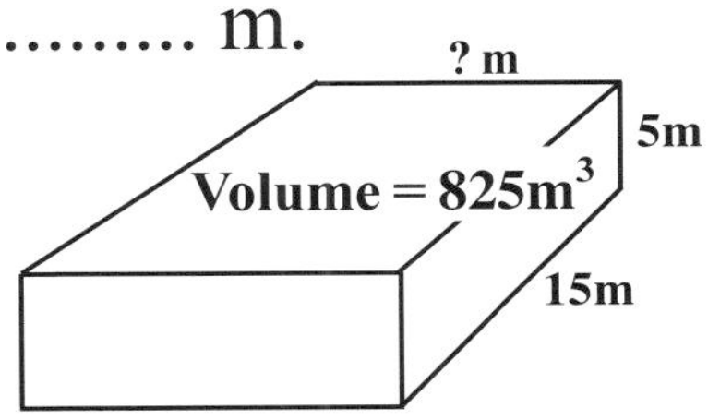

b) .... cm.

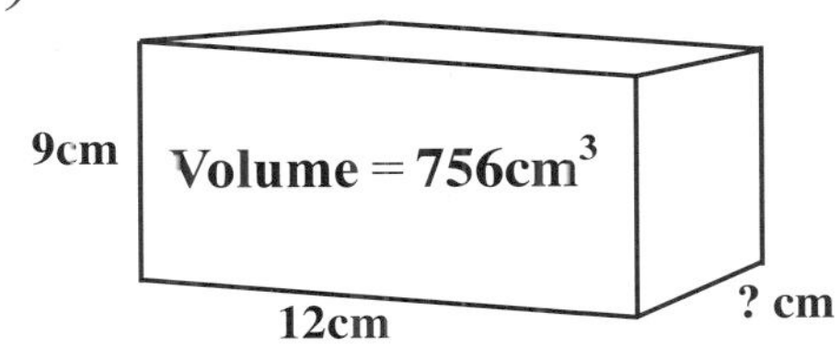

c. *Triangular Prisms*

The Volume of a Triangular Prism (Wedge) is half that of a Cuboid of the same Dimensions.

Example: Find the Volume:

Volume $= \frac{1}{2}$ **(Base × Height × Length)**

$= \frac{1}{2}\ (4 \times 4 \times 8)$

$= \frac{1}{2} \times 128$

The Volume is $64cm^3$.

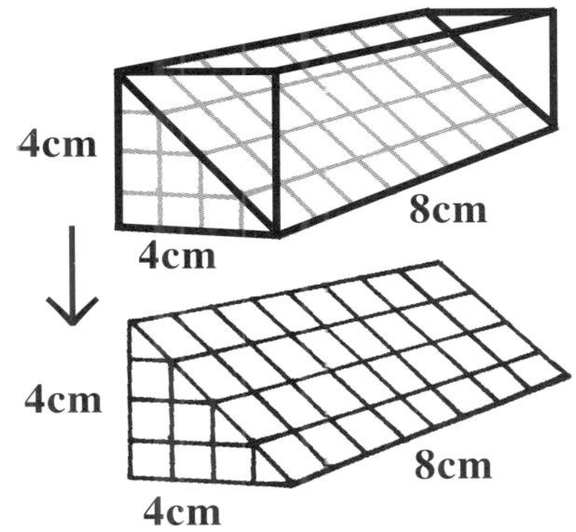

Exercise 16: 8f Find the Volume:

7) a)

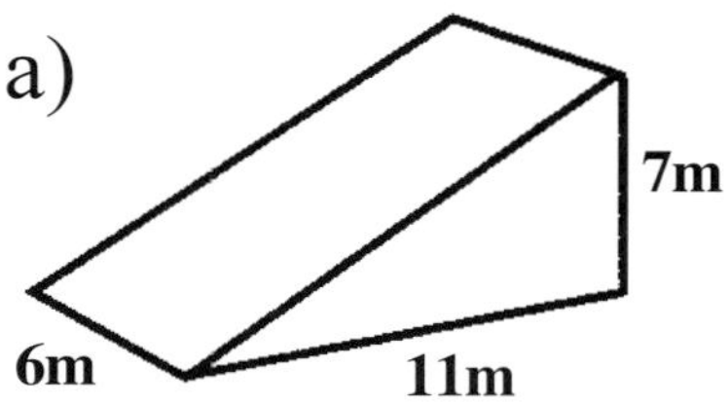

.... m^3.

b)

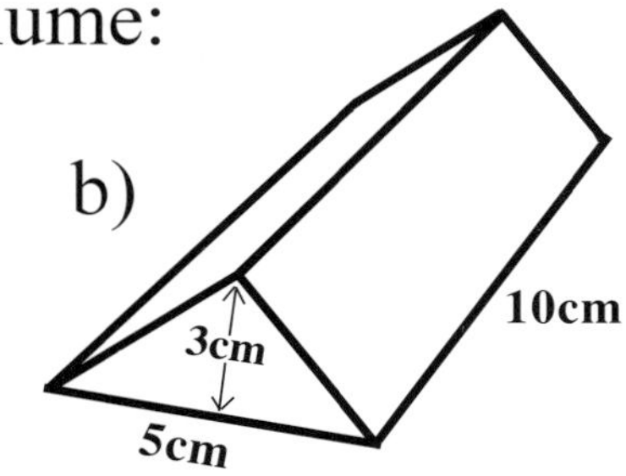

.... cm^3.

d. Circular Prisms (Cylinders)

Finding the Volume of Prisms:
Multiply Area of Top (Circle) by the Length

Example: Find the Volume:

Volume = $\pi \times r^2 \times$ **Length**

= $3.14 \times 3^2 \times 7$

= $3.14 \times 9 \times 7$

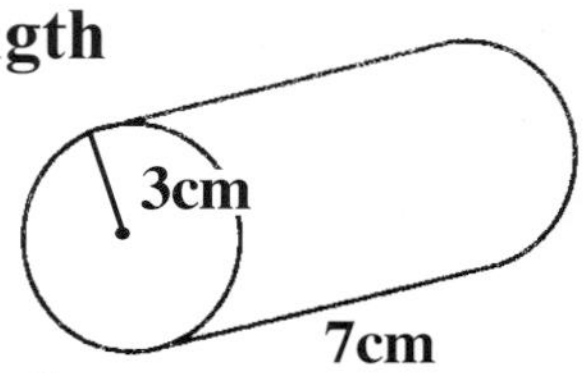

Volume is 197.82cm³.

Exercise 16: 8g

Find the Volume:

8)

Radius = **2cm**
Length = **4cm**

.... cm^3.

e. Capacity and Volume

Capacity and Volume are both ways of measuring the size of a 3-Dimensional space. The same units of measurement are used, but they indicate different things.

Capacity is a containing space or the room available to hold something.

Volume is the space actually taken up by an object.

Example: Explain the difference between Capacity and Volume using a **1.7 litre** coffee pot.

The empty coffee pot has a **Capacity** of **1.7 litres**.

The **Volume** of coffee needed to fill the pot is **1.7 litres**.

f. Volume and Weight (Mass)

There is a relationship between Volume and Weight (Mass). The basis of these Metric Measurements is water.

Example: How is the Volume and Weight of water in this **2 litre** jug related?

The jug holds **2 litres** of water.

The water (not the jug) weighs **2 kilograms**.

This only applies to water and no other substance.

Note - There is a scientific difference between Mass and Weight, but for Mathematical purposes at this level, the terms can be used interchangeably.

Exercise 16: 8h Calculate the following:

Score

9) A cask has a Capacity of (holds) **16.75ℓ** of water. The Mass of the cask when empty is **950g**. What is the Mass of the cask when it is full? .... kg.

10) The Weight of a bottle filled with water is **1.255kg**. The empty bottle weighs **455g**. Find the Volume of water in litres. .... litres.

5. Mensuration Problems

Exercise 16: 9 Calculate the following:

Use $\pi = \frac{22}{7}$

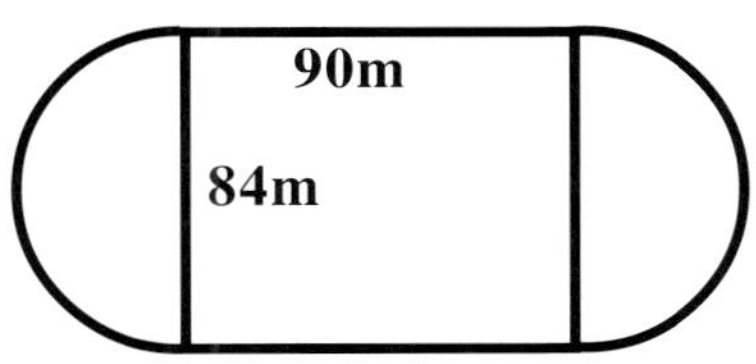

1) Find the Area of this field with Semi-circular ends .... m^2.

2) How many turns must the wheel of a bicycle with a Diameter of **0.7m** make to travel a distance of **44m**? (Find Circumference and Divide). Give your answer to the nearest whole turn. The wheel makes .... turns.

Use **3.14** for π

3) A garden is **50m** long and has an Area of **600m^2**. What is the Width? .... m.

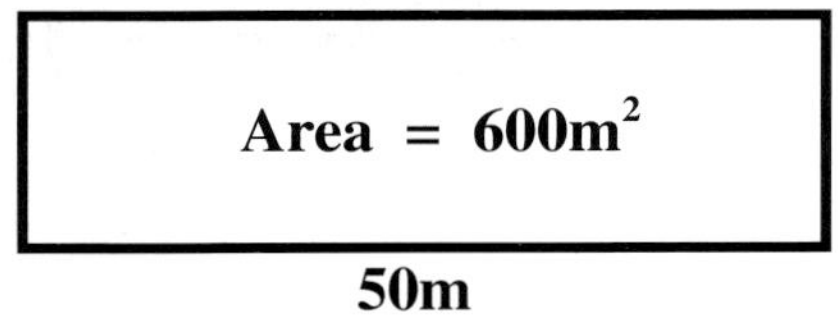

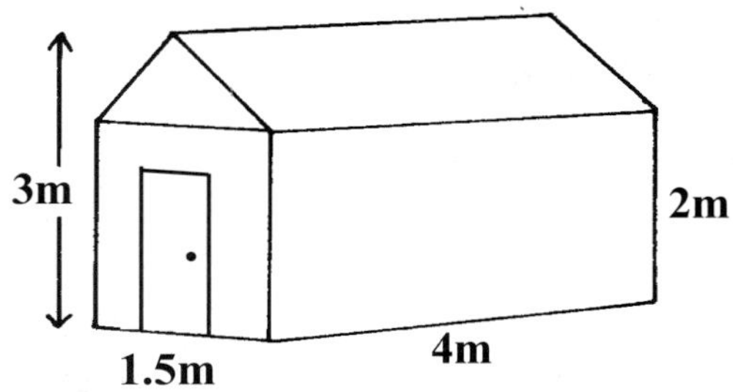

4) A man built a shed for his tools. The Volume of the shed is .... m^3.

5) Calculate the Area of each shaped flower bed. Round answers to the nearest whole number.

A = ... m^2.

B = ... m^2.

C = ... m^2.

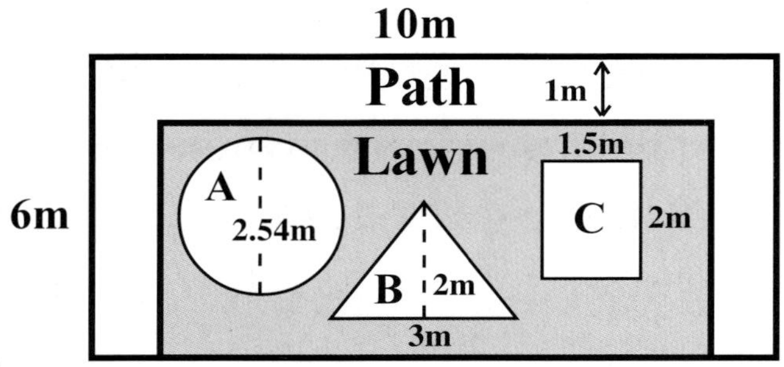

6) a) The Perimeter of the lawn is .... m.

b) The lawn Area is .... m^2.

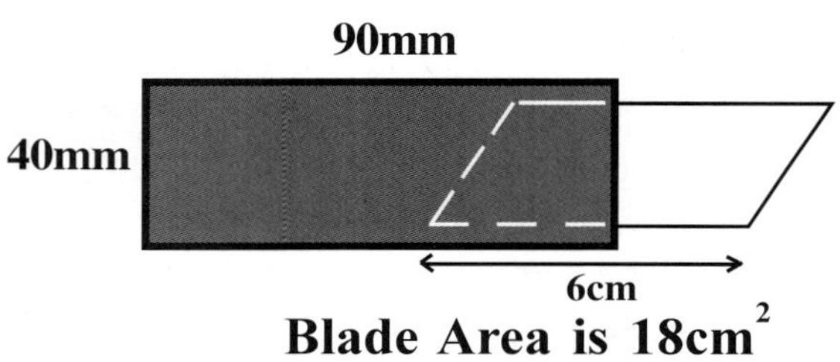

7) What is the Height of the blade of the knife? .... cm.

8) What is the Area of the handle? .... cm^2.

9) A small gift box contains a number of fine chocolates. What is the Perimeter of the box? .... cm.

10) What is the Area of each chocolate in the box? Give your answers to 2 decimal places.

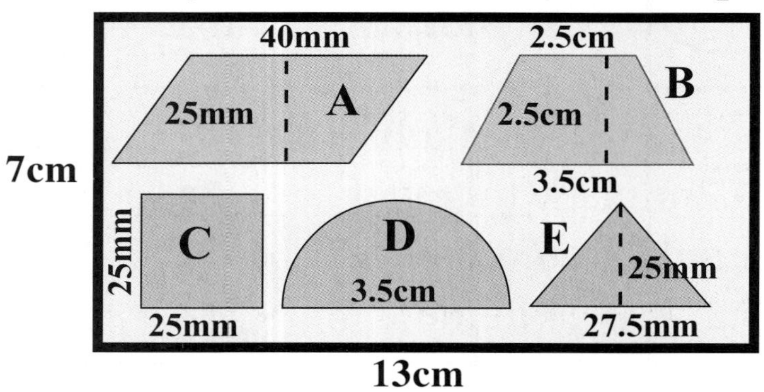

A = ... cm^2.

B = ... cm^2.

C = ... cm^2.

D = ... cm^2.

E = ... cm^2.

Score

Chapter Seventeen

GEOMETRY

1. Transformations

Transformations are 2D Shape movements. There are four kinds of Transformation. The new Shape is called an **Image**.

Translation **Reflection** **Rotation** **Enlargement**

a. Translation

Translation occurs when a Shape **Slides** from one position to another. It should not be turned around or flipped over.

Example:

Translate **Shape A** by **4** Squares to the right and **4** Squares down.

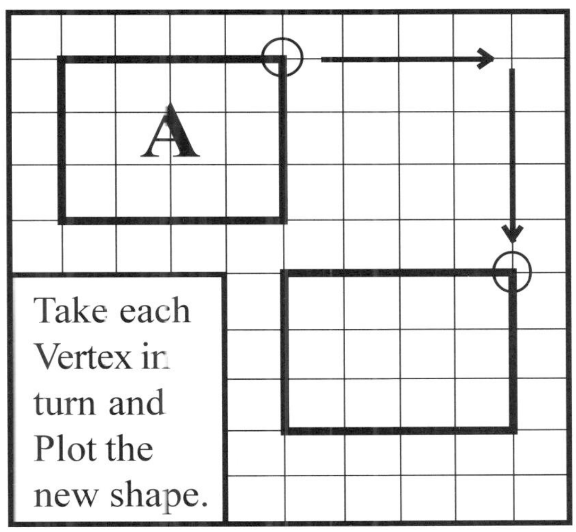

Exercise 17: 1a Translate the following Shapes:

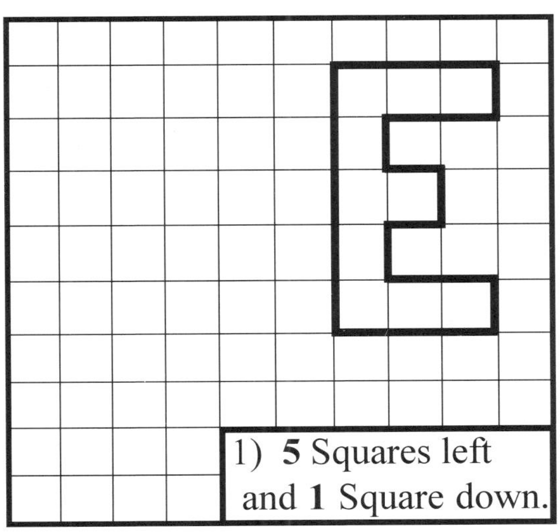

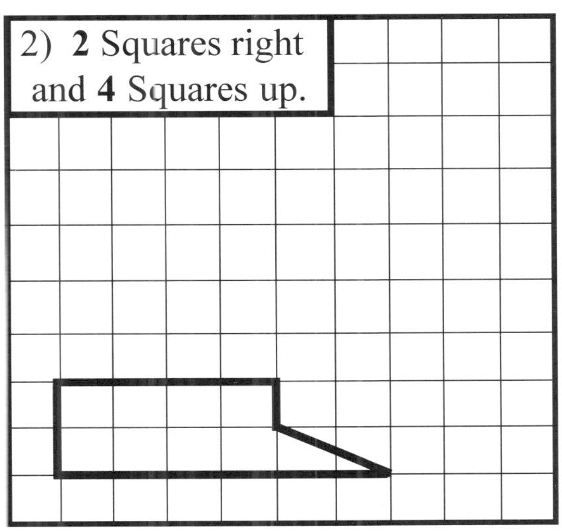

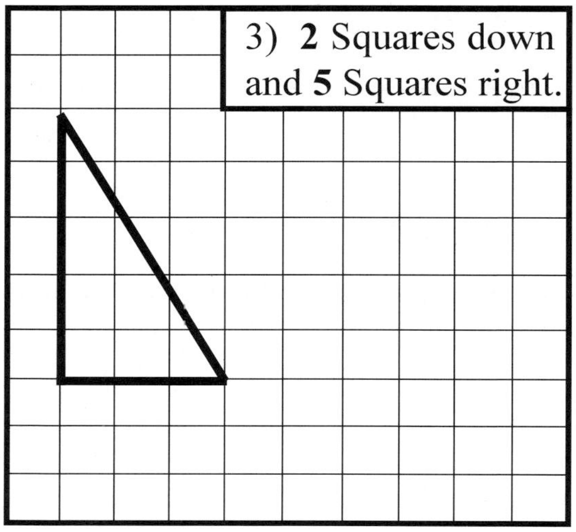

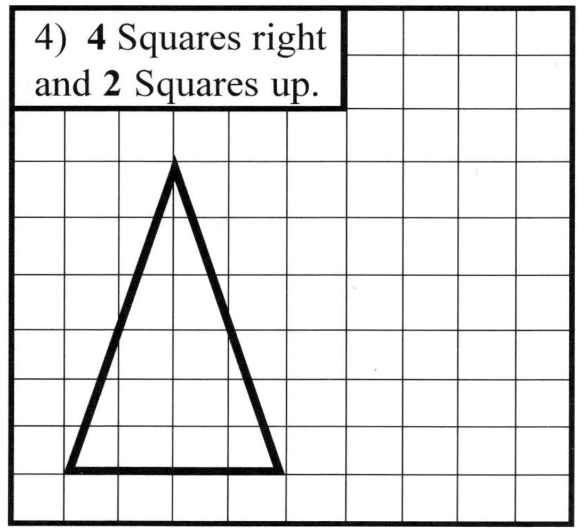

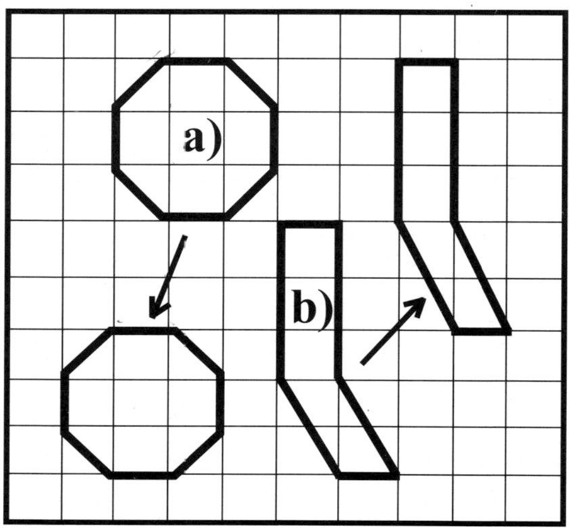

The following Shapes have been Translated by:

5) a) .... squares .... and .... square ....

b) .... squares .... and .... squares ....

b. Reflection

Shapes can be Reflected by marking the same points on the other side of the dotted line. This is the **Mirror Line** (If a mirror is placed along the Mirror Line you would see this Reflection).

Example:

Reflect **Shape A** in the Mirror Line to form **Shape B**.

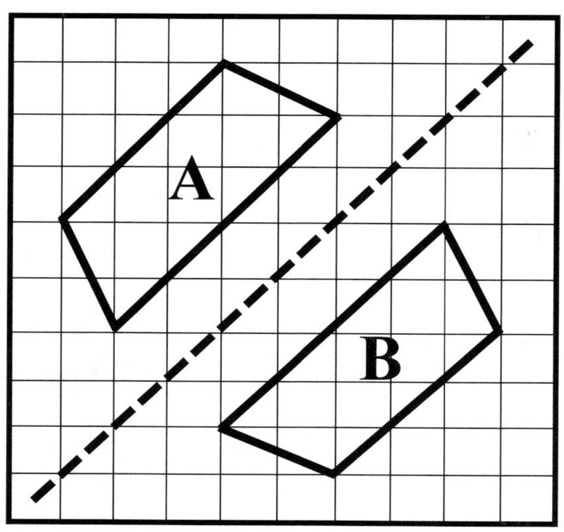

Exercise 17: 1b Reflect the following Shapes:

6)

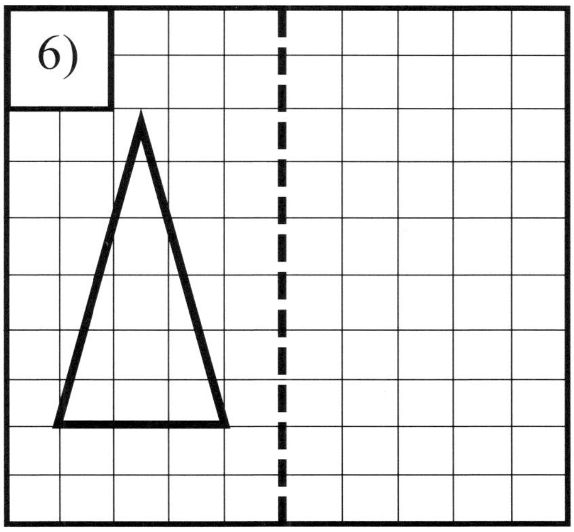

7)

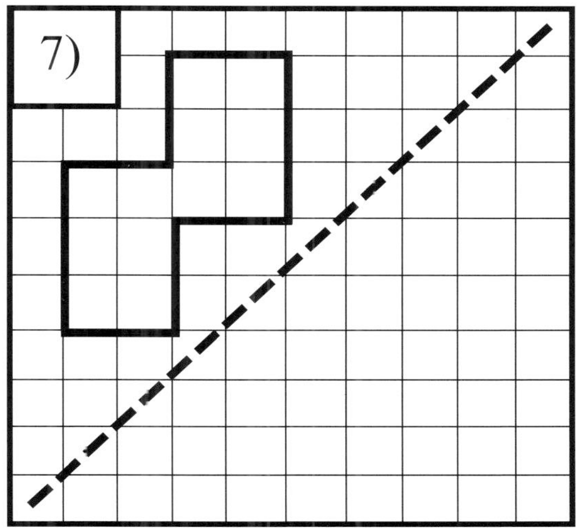

8)

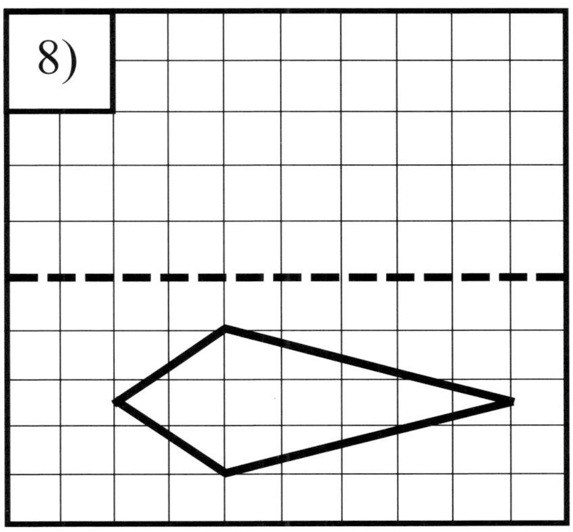

9)

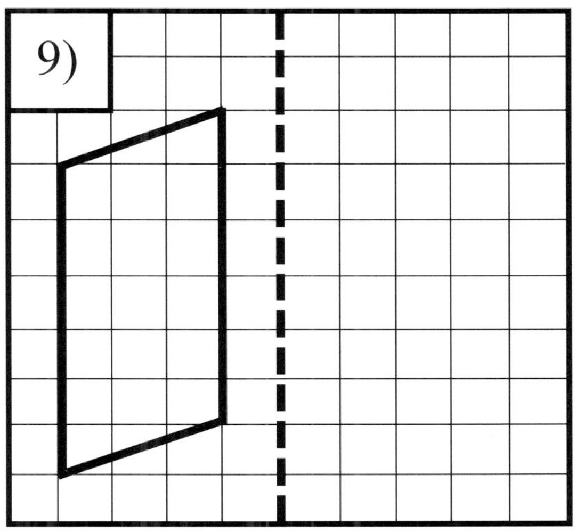

10)

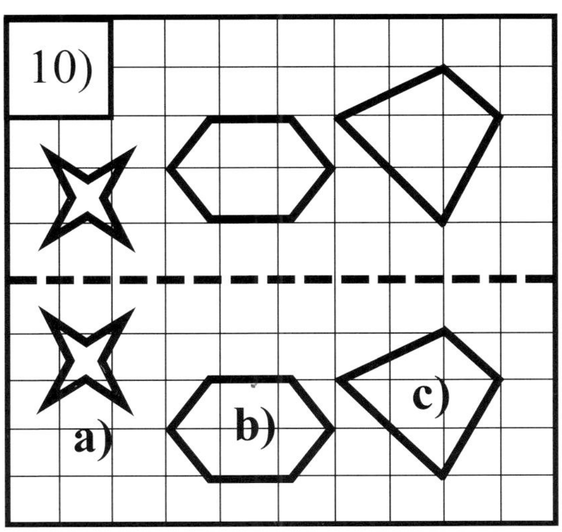

Have the following Shapes been Reflected? Underline the correct answer.

10) a) True/False

b) True/False

c) True/False

Score

c. Rotation

A Shape can be Rotated about a point by Turns or Degrees (e.g. 90°). It can Rotate Clockwise (positive) or Anti-clockwise (negative). Plot each new Vertex one at a time. Join the dots to draw the Shape.
Example:

Rotate the Shape in $\frac{1}{4}$ Turns.

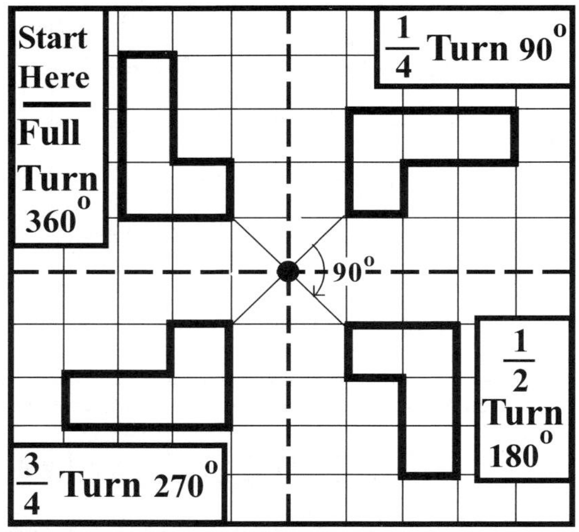

Exercise 17: 2a Rotate the following Shapes:

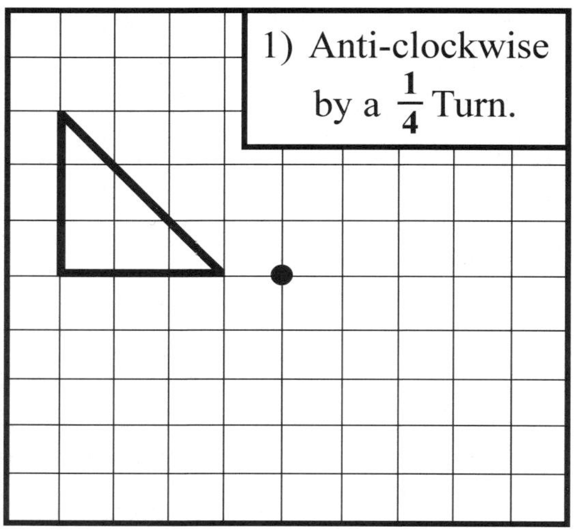

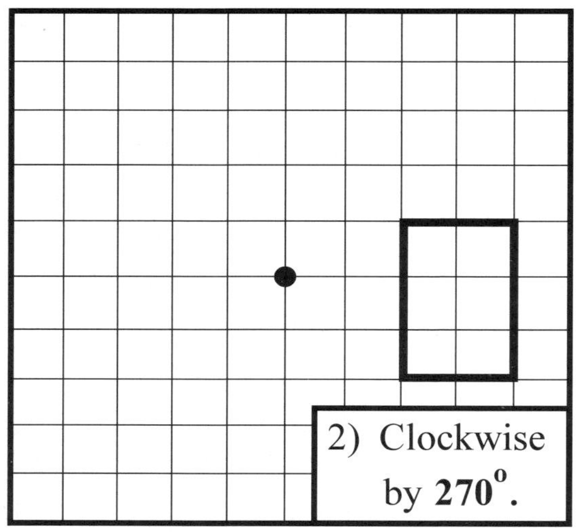

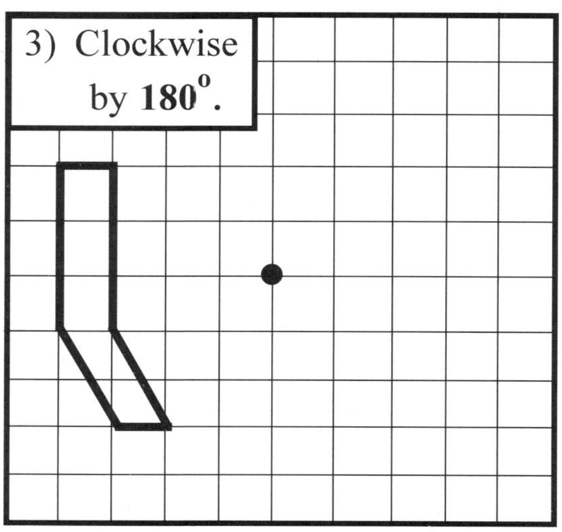

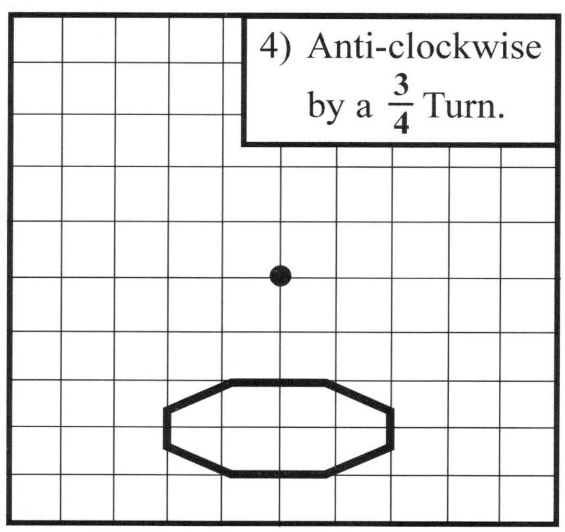

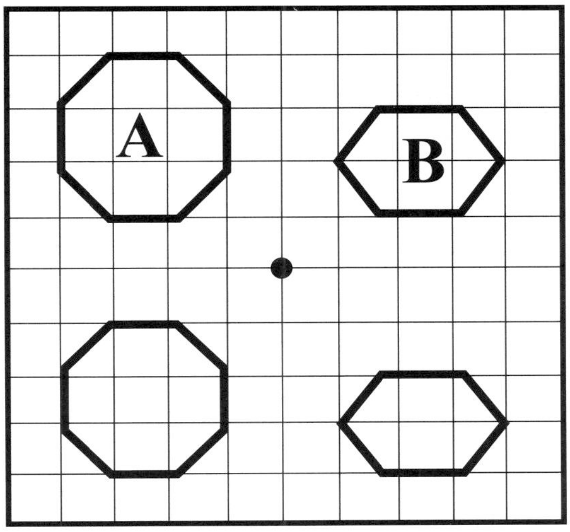

5) a) By how many Degrees has Shape **A** been **Rotated Clockwise**?

...........^{o}

b) Has Shape **B** been **Rotated**? Yes or No? Underline the correct answer.

d. Enlargement

Enlarging by the **Ray Method.**

1. **Draw lines**

   From the Centre of Enlargement out through all the Vertices of the Shape.

2. **Multiply**

   Distance from Centre of Enlargement to the object. $\times$ Scale Factor (How many times Enlarged).

   $2 \times 2 = 4$ squares

3. **Draw New Object**

   Use the lines to help.

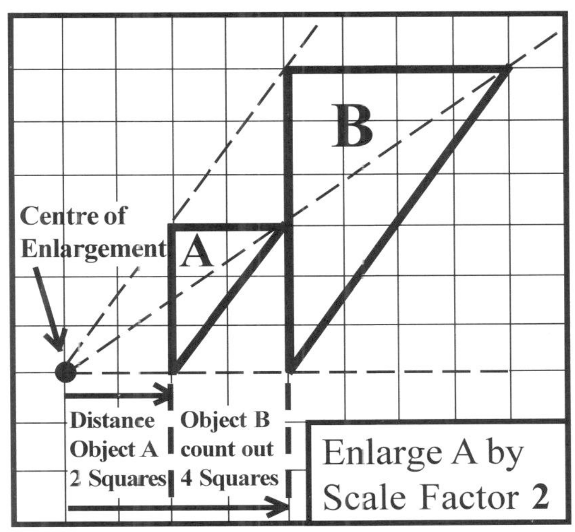

Exercise 17: 2b

Enlarge the following Shapes:

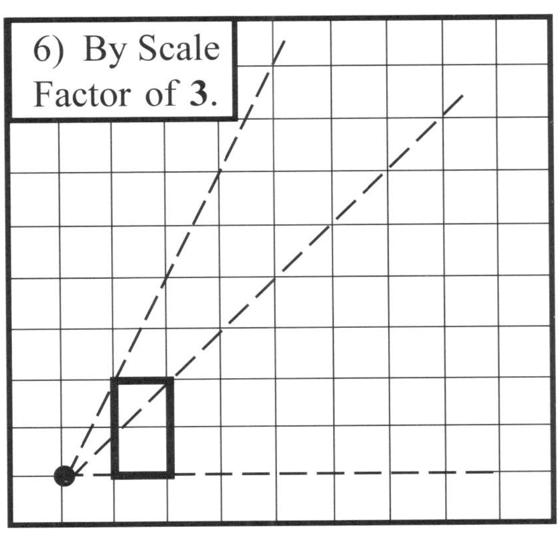

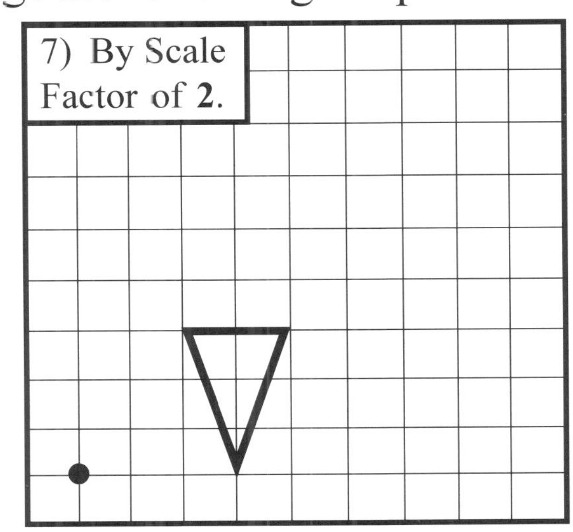

Enlarging by the **Coordinate Method**.

1. Count the Squares

Count from the Centre of Enlargement to each point in the first Shape e.g. **Point a** is (2 along and 3 up).

2. Multiply

Multiply each Dimension by the Scale Factor of 2 e.g. **Point b** becomes (4 along and 6 up).

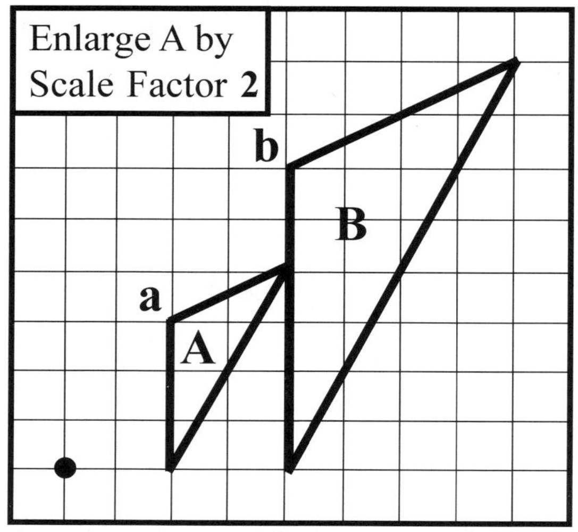

Exercise 17: 2c

Enlarge the following Shapes using the Coordinate Method:

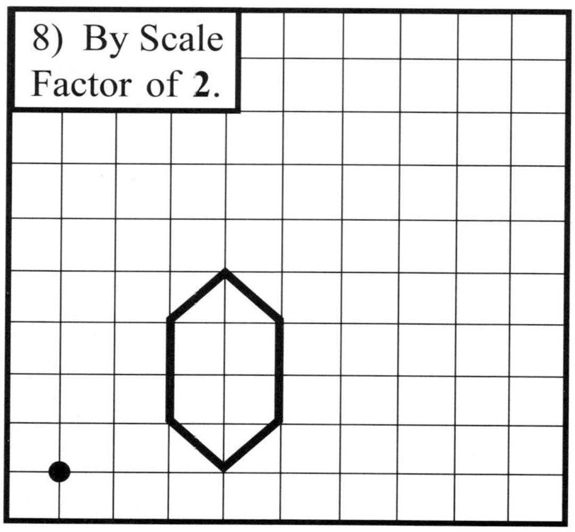

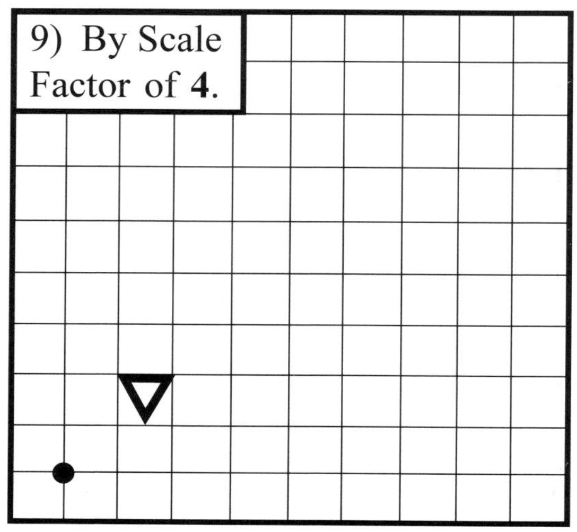

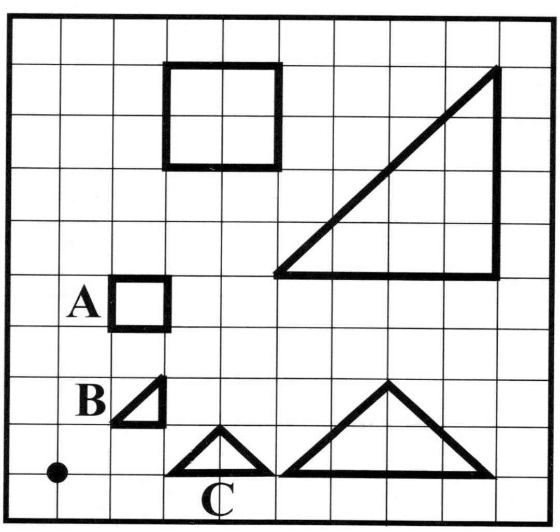

10) The Shapes are Enlarged by Scale Factors:

a) Shape **A** - Scale Factor of ....

b) Shape **B** - Scale Factor of ....

c) Shape **C** - Scale Factor of ....

Score

2. Topological Transformations

Shapes are Topologically Equivalent (will Transform) if when **Deformed** they retain the same number of Vertices, Edges and Faces. The Vertices or Points along each Edge should follow the same order.

Example:

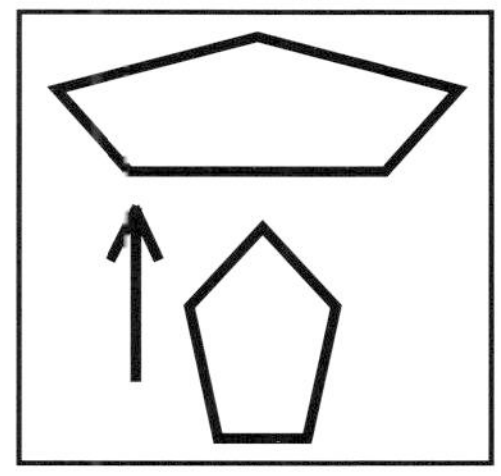

Exercise 17: 3 Do the Shapes Transform? Yes or No.

Score

1) 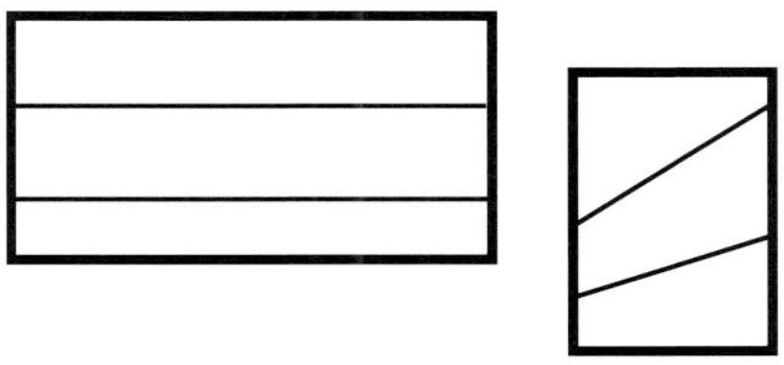

______

2) 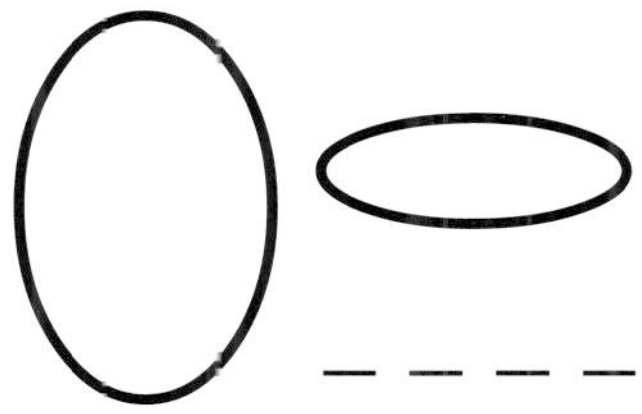

______

3) 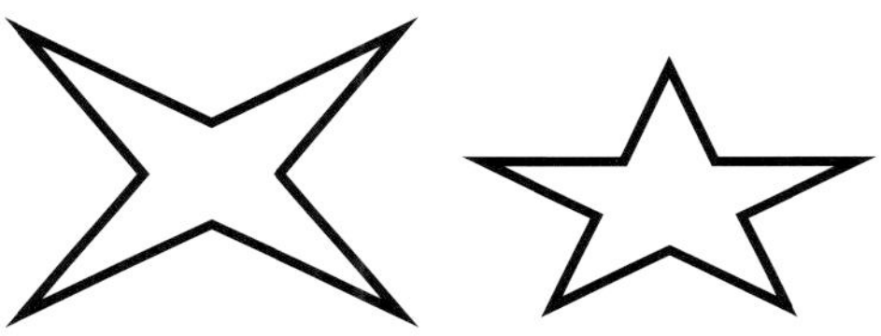

______

4) 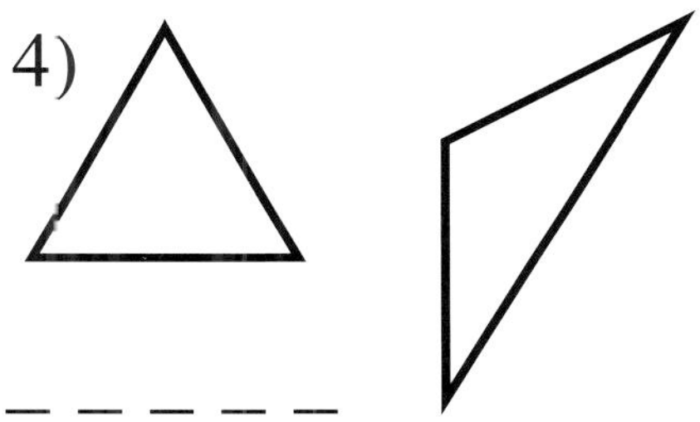

______

5) 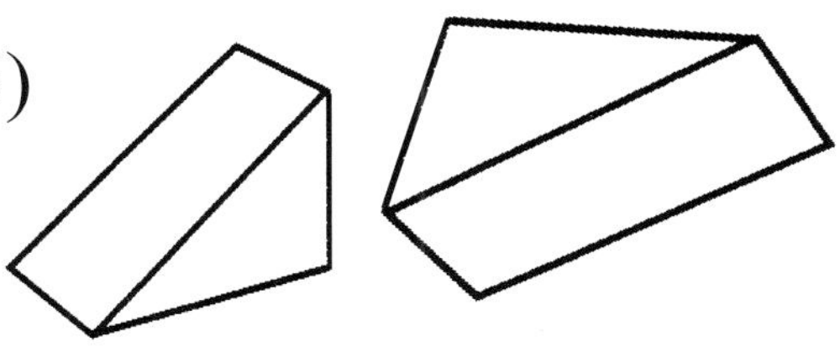

______

6) 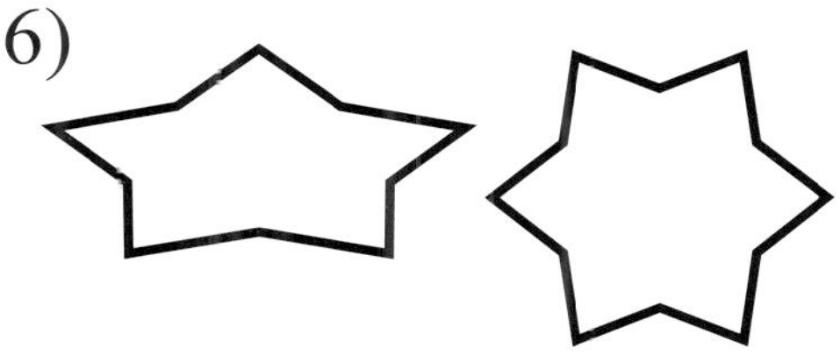

______

7) 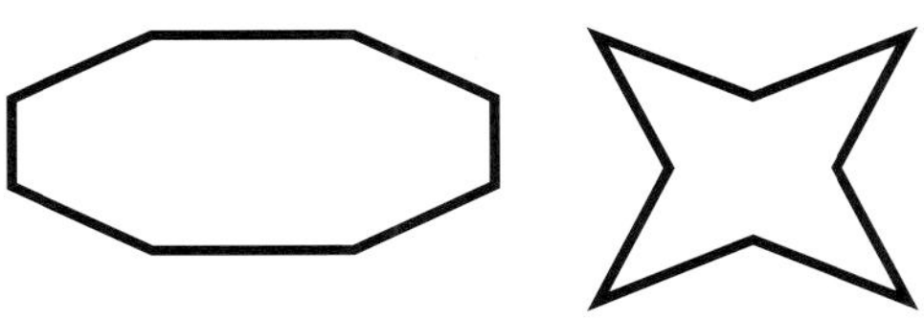

______

8) 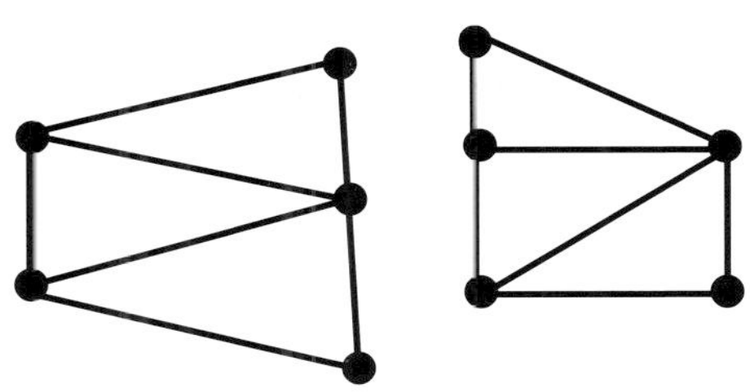

______

9) 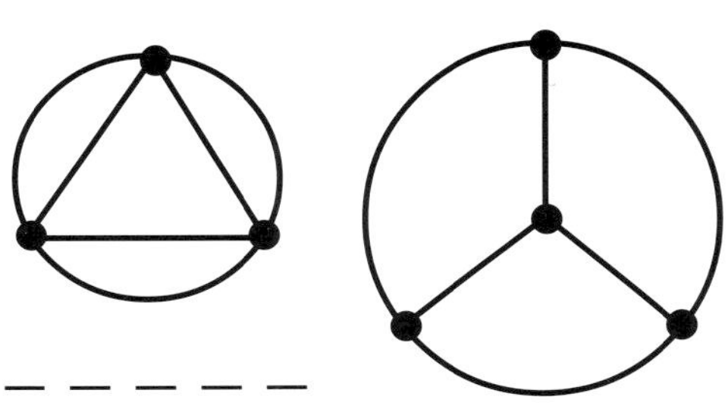

______

10) 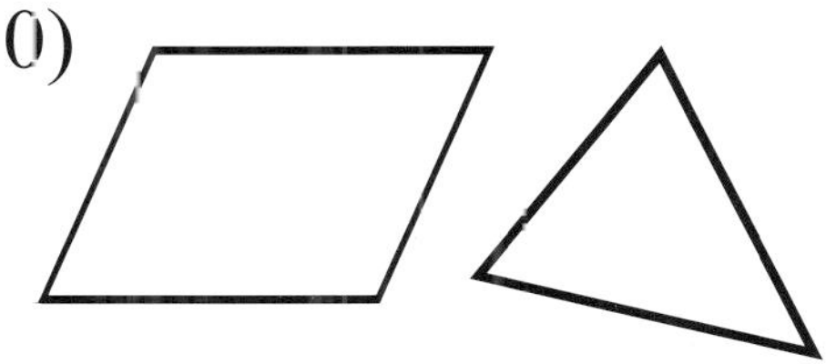

______

3. Congruency and Similarity

When two Shapes are **Congruent** they are exactly the Same Size and Shape.

Example:

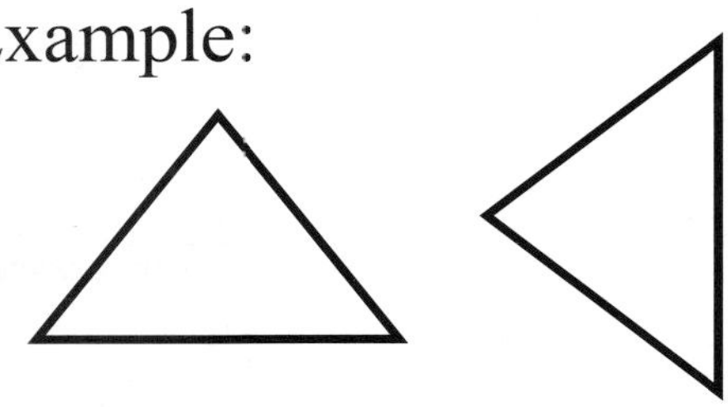

These Shapes are Identical even though one has been Rotated.

When two Shapes are **Similar** they are the Same Shape but of a Different Size. The size of the angles and number of Sides is the same.

Example:

These Shapes are the Same except one is smaller.

Exercise 17: 4 Answer the following:

1) Which Shapes are Congruent?

....

2) Which Shapes are Similar?

....

3) Which Shapes are Different? ....

In the following, find the one that is Different (**not** Similar).

4) 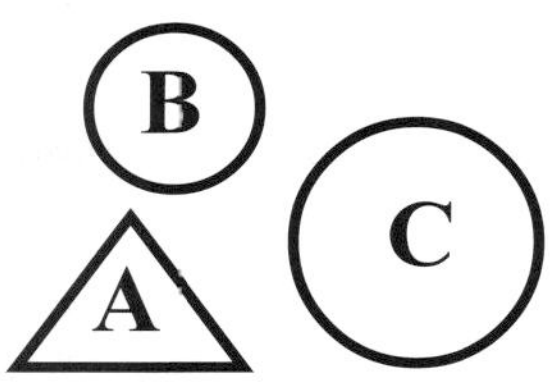

....

5) 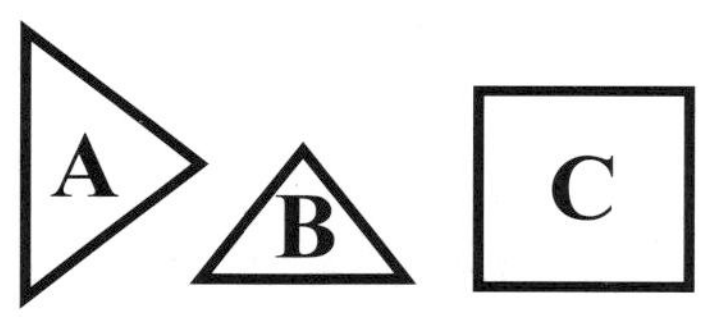

....

6) 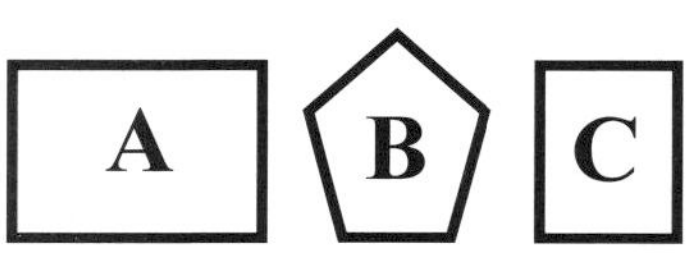

....

7) 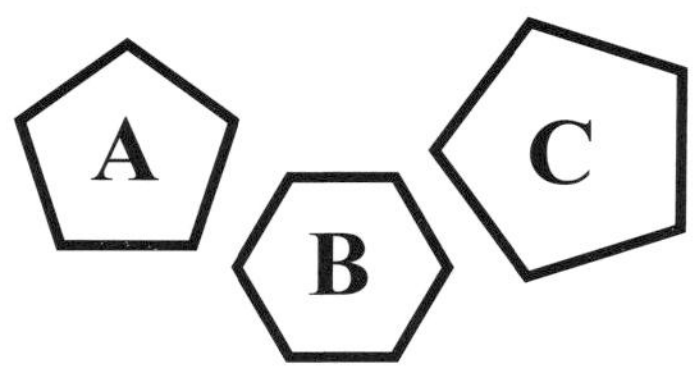

....

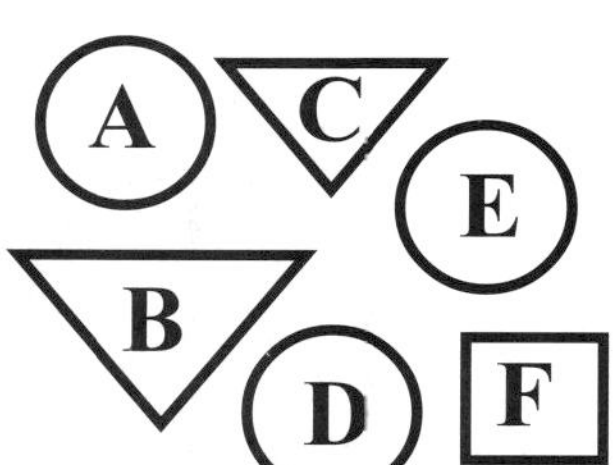

8) Which Shapes are Congruent?

....

9) Which Shapes are Similar?

....

10) Which Shape is Different? ....

Score

4. Tessellations

Tessellating shapes fit together without gaps. Examples:

These Hexagons are Tessellating Shapes.

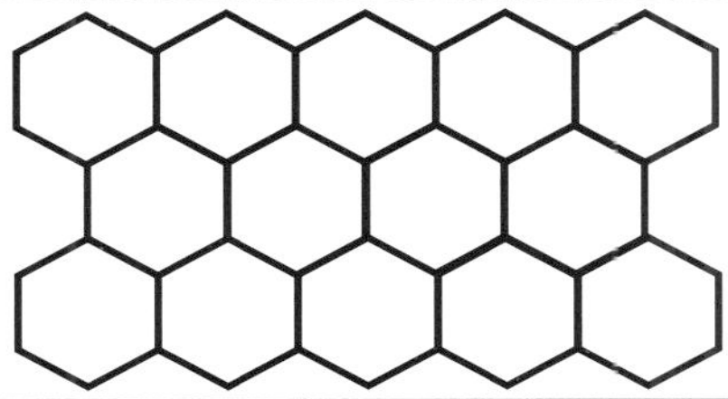

These Circles will not Tessellate.

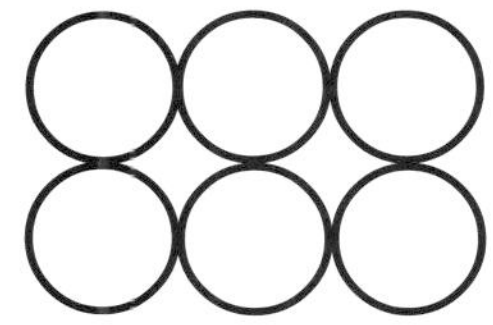

Exercise 17: 5a Do the following Shapes Tessellate?

1)

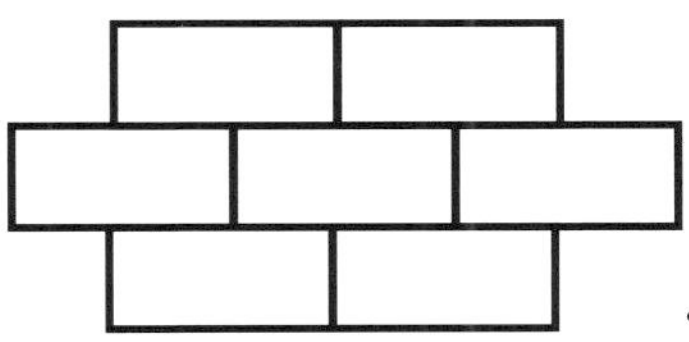

....

2)

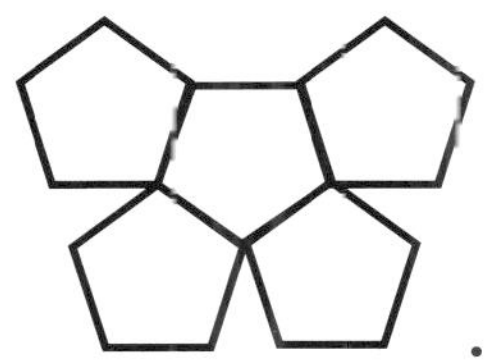

....

3)

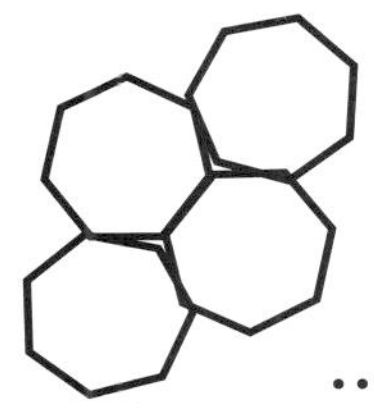

....

4) Will this Shape Tessellate? Yes or no? (Test it) ....

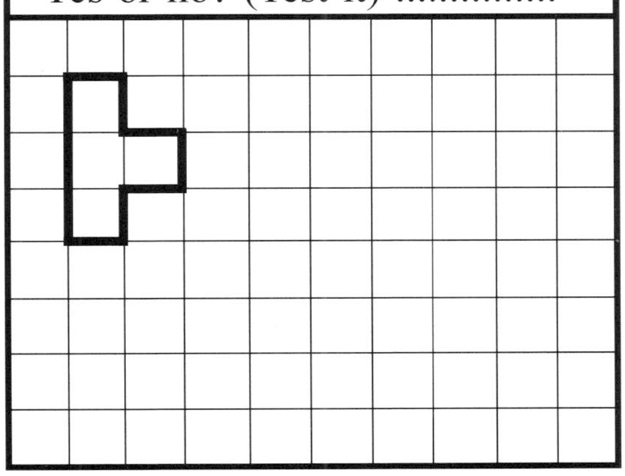

5) Draw a Tessellation for this Triangle within the outline given.

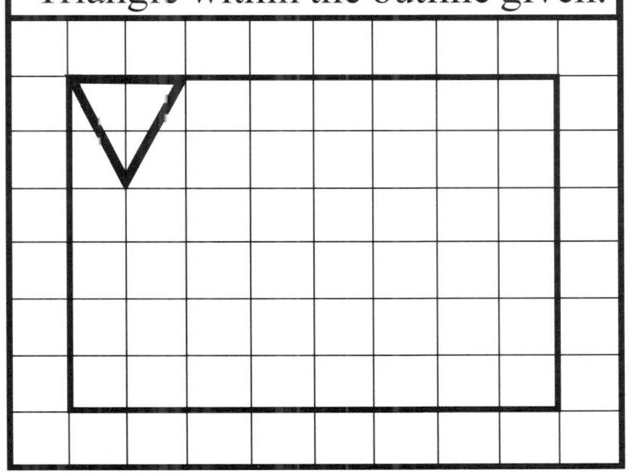

5. Networks

A Network is a set of Points joined by Lines that are never broken. A Network is **Transversable** if it can be drawn as one Continuous Line without going over any Line more than once. Examples:

Transversable
You can trace the circle with a pencil and then the Triangle in one continuous movement.

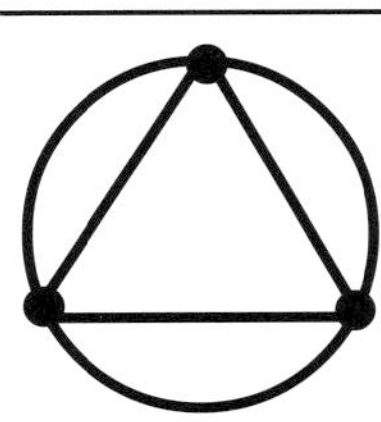

Not Transversable
You cannot trace the Shape in one continuous movement without going over one of the Lines again.

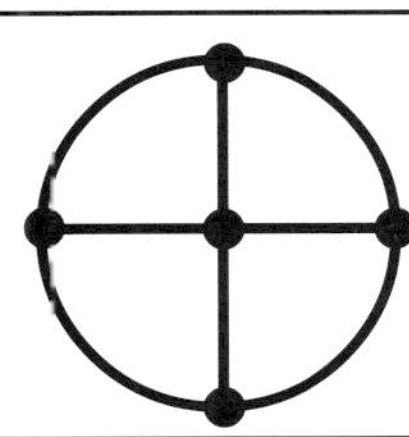

Exercise 17: 5b Are these Networks Transversable? Yes or No.

6) 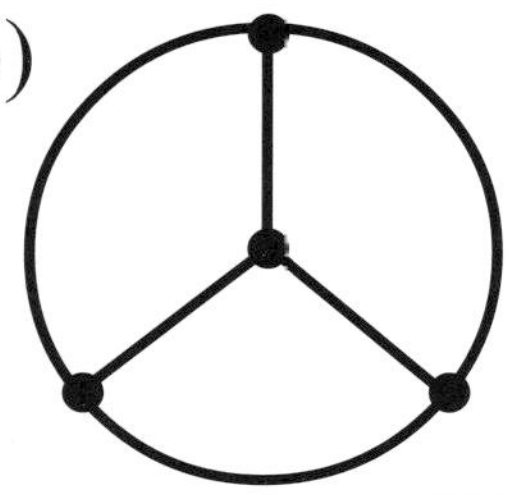 ....

7) 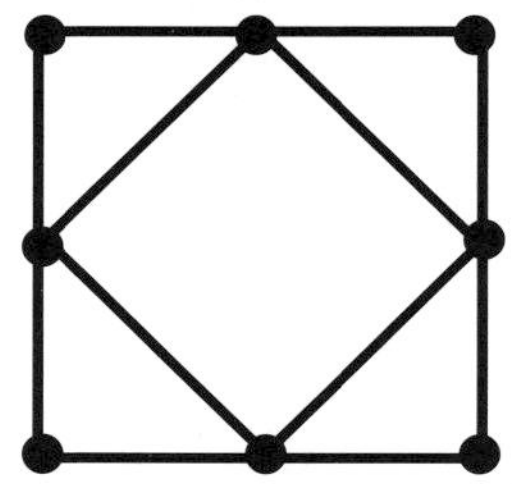 ....

8) 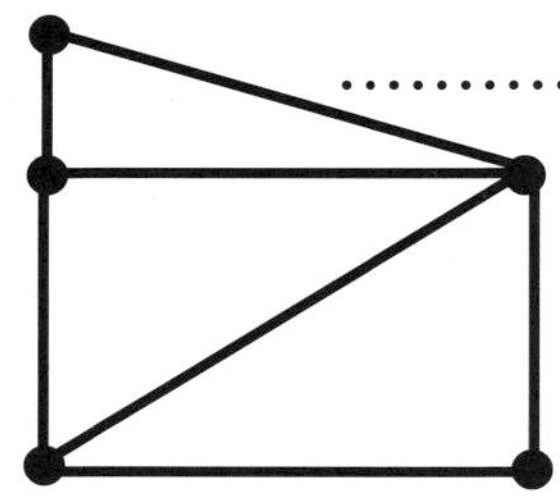 ....

9) a) How far is it from C to D and back to C again by the shortest route? ...... units

b) Is this Network Transversable? ....

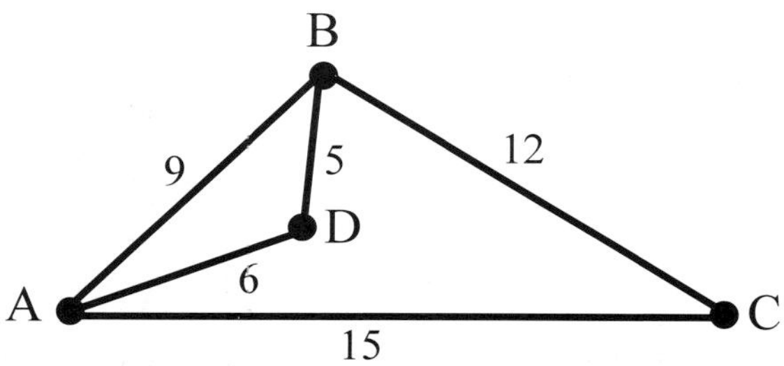

10) a) The shortest Distance from A to D is ..... units.

b) What would the Distance be if Points A to F are visited in order? ..... units.

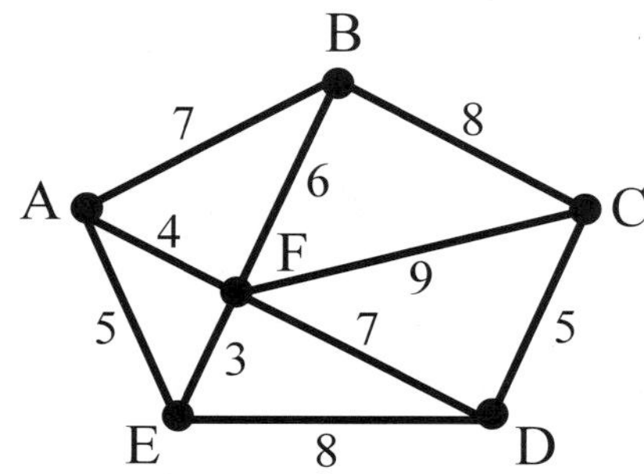

Score

6. Coordinate Systems

a. Grid References

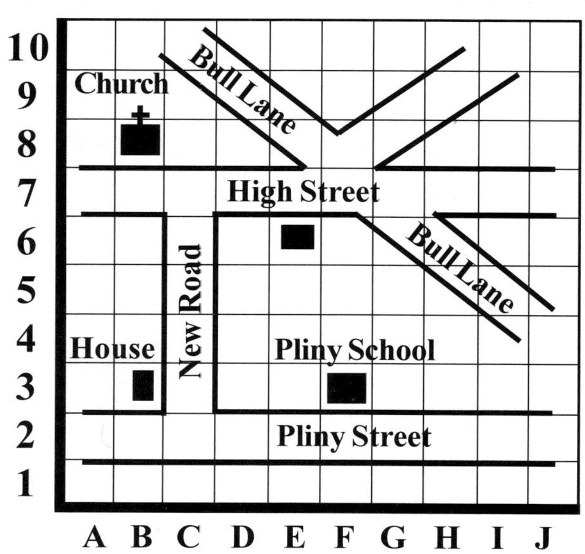

Grid References make use of Horizontal Rows and Vertical Columns to locate an object. References are given by Column (usually letters) and then by Row (usually numbers).

Examples:

Church is at **B8**	House is at **B3**
School is at **F3**	Shop is at **E6**

Exercise 17: 6a

1a) <u>Give References</u> for:

i) The Circle ....

ii) The Triangle ....

iii) The Pentagon ....

<u>Draw</u> the following:

iv) A Square at **0307**

v) A Cross at **0503**

vi) A Rectangle at **0203**

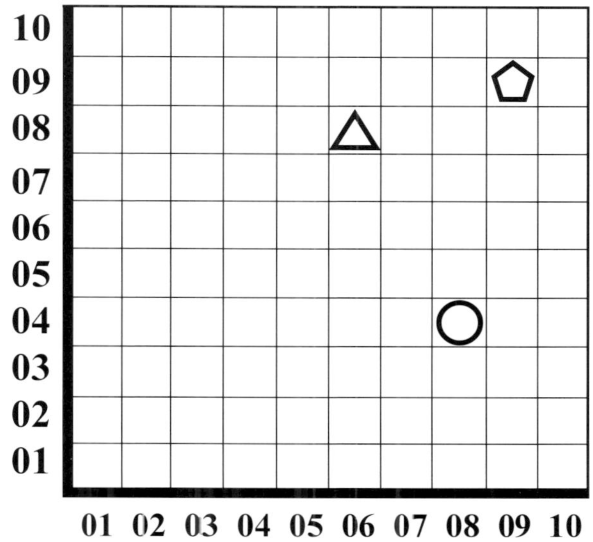

1b) <u>Give Approximate</u> <u>References</u> for:

i) The Wreck ....

ii) The Rocks ....

iii) The Forest ....

iv) The pirates have to find the Treasure from the spot marked **x**.

'**3** Squares west, **4** Squares south, **4** Squares east, **2** Squares south' ....

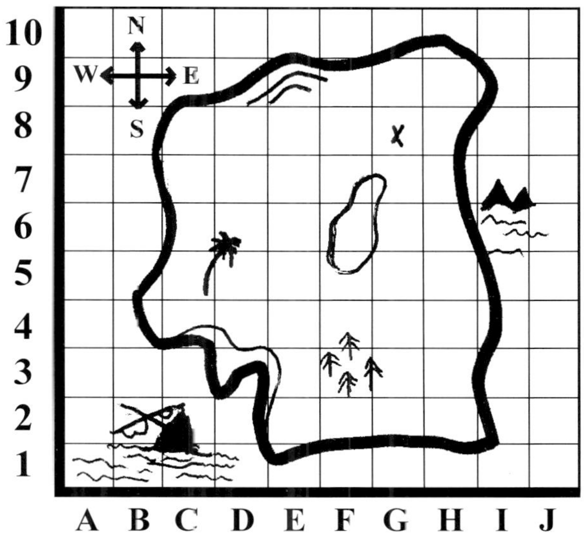

b. First Quadrant Coordinates

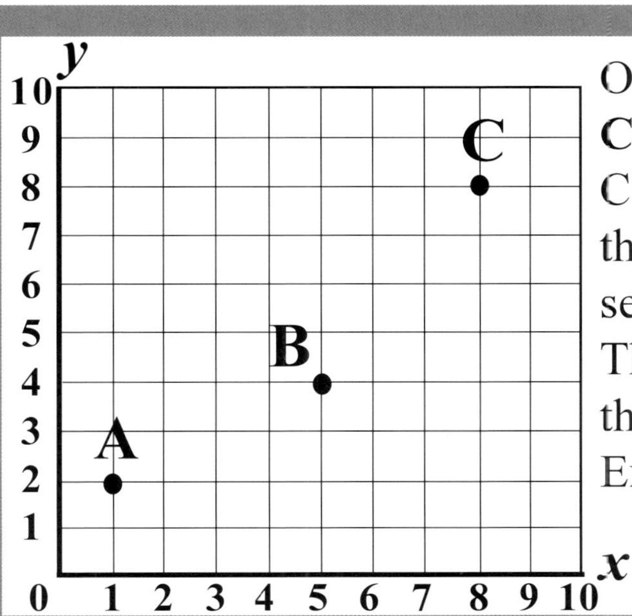

Objects can be found using **Coordinate Maps**. The first Coordinate number refers to the Horizontal ***x*-axis** and the second to the Vertical ***y*-axis**. This is an **Ordered Pair** as they must be in this order.

Example: Write Coordinates for letters **A**, **B** & **C**.

A = **(1, 2)**; **B** = **(5, 4)**; **C** = **(8, 8)**

Exercise 17: 6b

2) Mark the Coordinates and join them up to make Shapes.

a) (1, 9) (3, 5) (7, 9) (9, 5)
This Shape is a

....

b) (1, 1) (5, 4) (9, 1)
This Shape is an

....

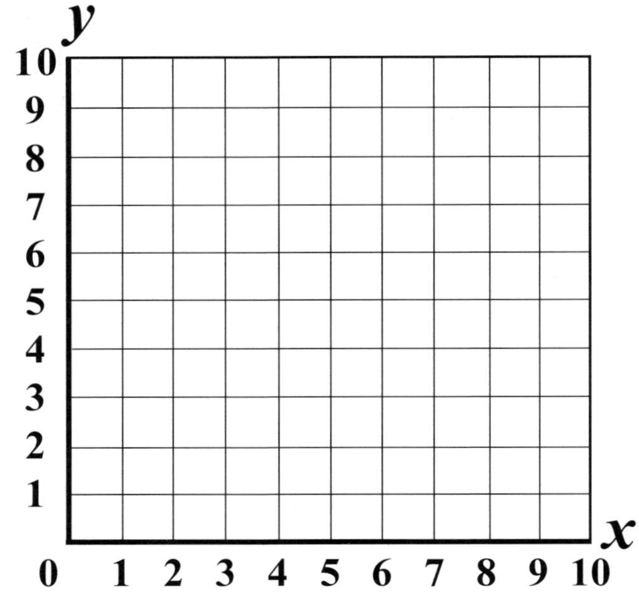

3) Write the Coordinates of the following Shapes:

a) A = (   ) B = (   )
C = (   ) D = (   )
E = (   ) F = (   )

b) G = (   ) H = (   )
I = (   )

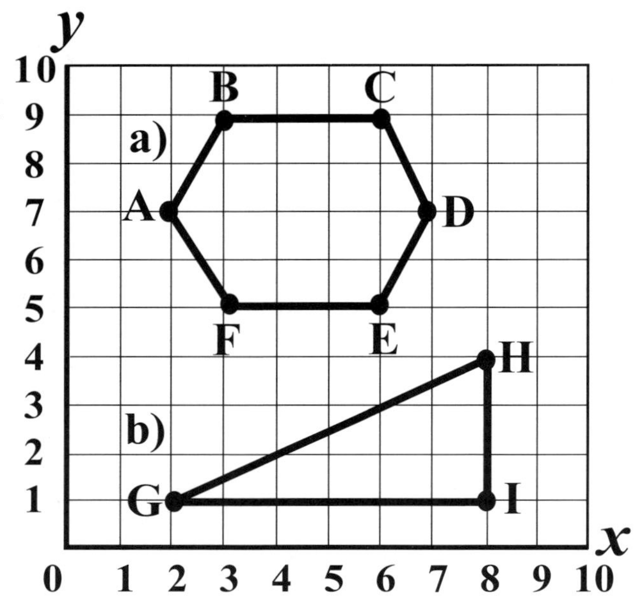

4) Write the Coordinates of this Shape.

a) A = (   ) B = (   )
C = (   ) D = (   )
E = (   )

b) Draw a Reflection of the Shape and write the new Coordinates.
A1 = (   ) B1 = (   )
C1 = (   ) D1 = (   )
E1 = (   )

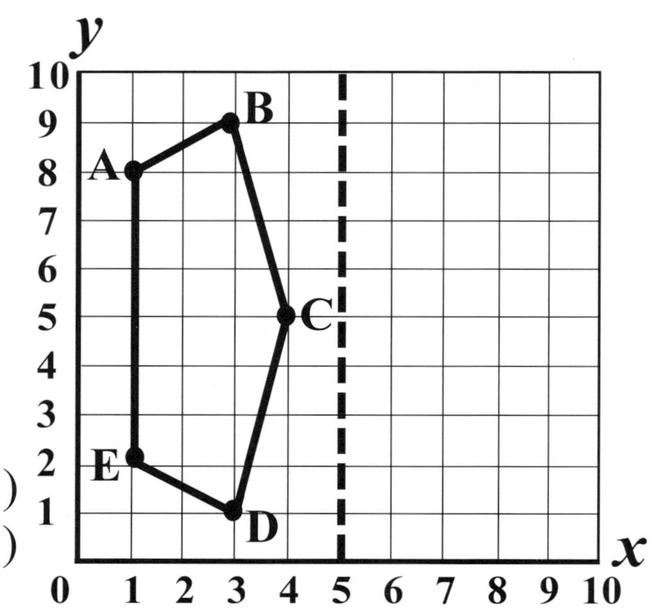

5) Mark the Coordinates and join them up to make Shapes.

a) (2, 5) (8, 5) (4, 9) (8, 9)
This Shape is a

....

b) (2, 1) (9, 1) (2, 4) (9, 4)
This Shape is a

....

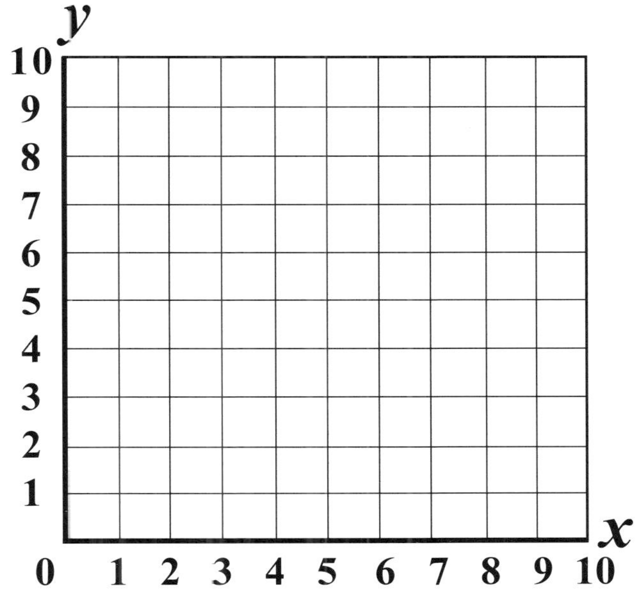

6) Write the Coordinates of these Shapes:

a) A = ( ) B = ( )
C = ( ) D = ( )
E = ( ) F = ( )

b) G = ( ) H = ( )
I = ( )

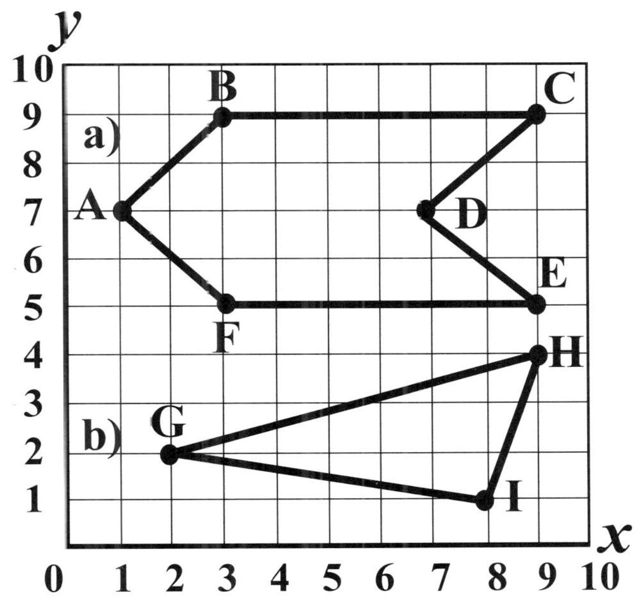

7) Write the Coordinates of this Shape.

a) A = ( ) B = ( )
C = ( ) D = ( )
E = ( )

b) If this shape is Reflected, the new Coordinates will be?
A1 = ( ) B1 = ( )
C1 = ( ) D1 = ( )
E1 = ( )

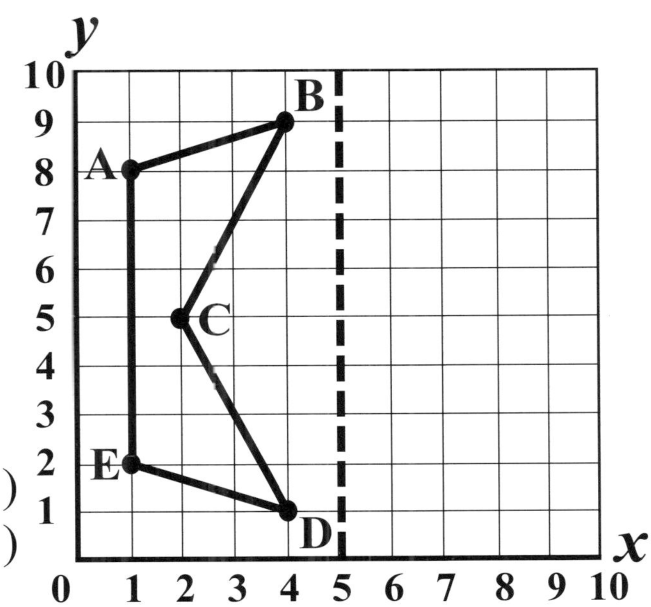

c. Positive and Negative Coordinates

Coordinates in all Four Quadrants are created by extending the ***x*-axis** (Horizontal) left along from **0** and the ***y*-axis** (Vertical) down from **0**. The point zero (**0, 0**) is called the **Origin**. The Graph is always read ***x*-axis first** and ***y*-axis second**.

(Think - 'along the corridor left or right and then up or down the stairs').

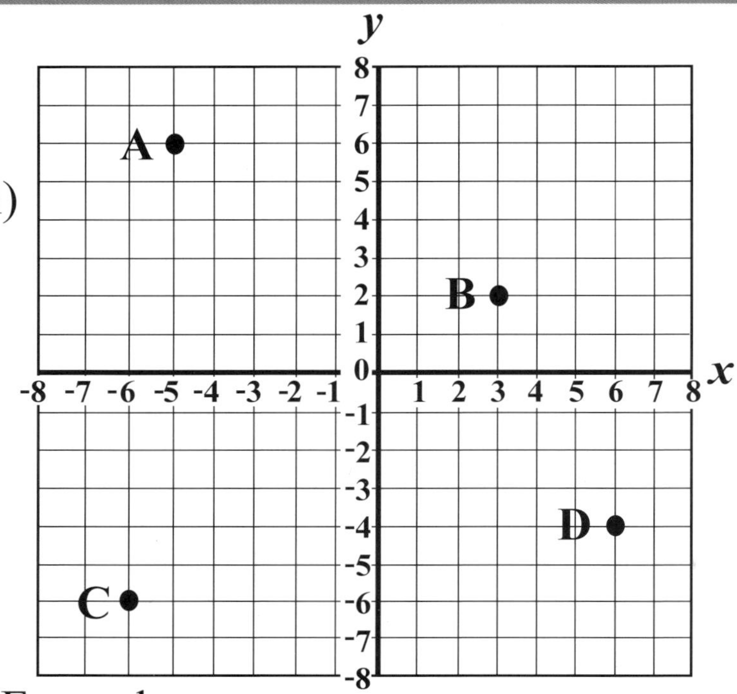

Example:

Give the Coordinates for **A, B, C, D.**

A = **(-5, 6)** **B** = **(3, 2)** **C** = **(-6, -6)** **D** = **(6, -4)**

Exercise 17: 6c Work out the following:

8a) Plot the Coordinates and join the dots to find the Shapes.

i) **(-6, 6)** **(2, 6)** **(-6, -2)** **(2, -2)**

This is a ....

ii) **(3, 1)** **(5, 4)** **(7, 1)** **(7, -4)** **(5, -7)** **(3, -4)**

This is an ....

....

iii) **(-6, -4)** **(-3, -4)** **(-2, -7)** **(-7, -7)**

This is an ....

....

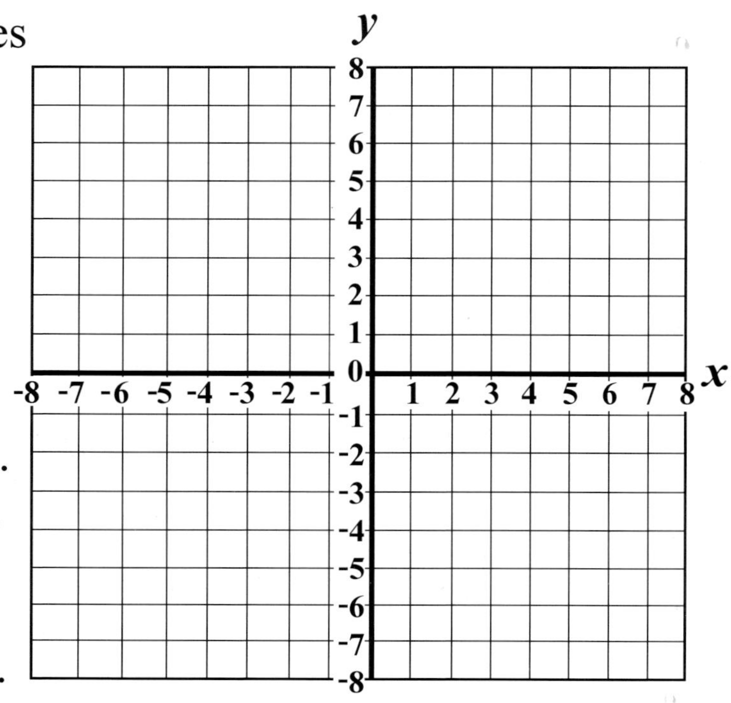

8b) Plot the Coordinates and join the dots to find the Shapes.

i) (-7, 1) (-3, 1) (-3, 5) (-5, 7) (-7, 5)

This shape is a

....

ii) (5, 5) (7, 5) (2, -4) (4, -4)

This shape is a

....

iii) (-2, -2) (-7, -6) (-4, -7)

This shape is a

....

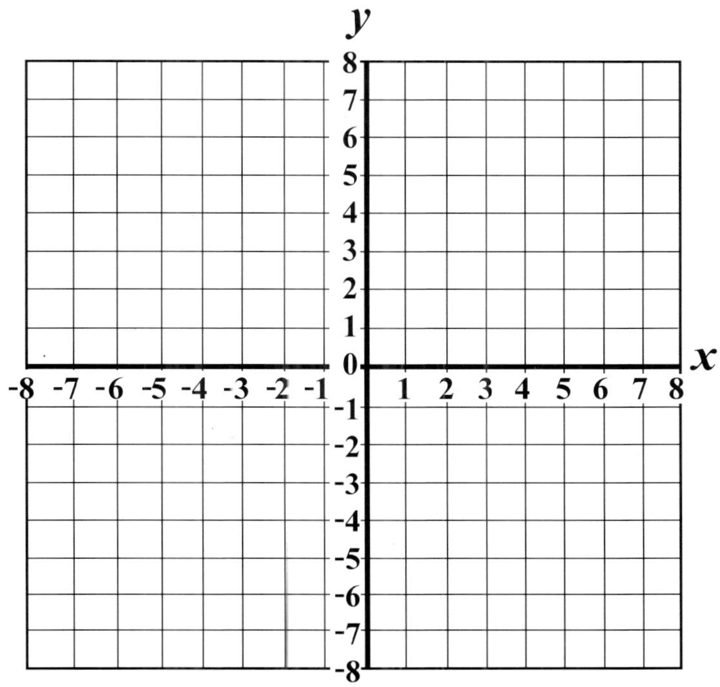

8c) Write Coordinates for the following Shapes and Lines.

i) A = ( ) B = ( )
C = ( ) D = ( )
E = ( ) F = ( )

This shape is a

....

ii) G = ( ) H = ( )

This Line is a

....

iii) I = ( ) J = ( )

This Line is

....

iv) K = ( ) L = ( )

This Line is

....

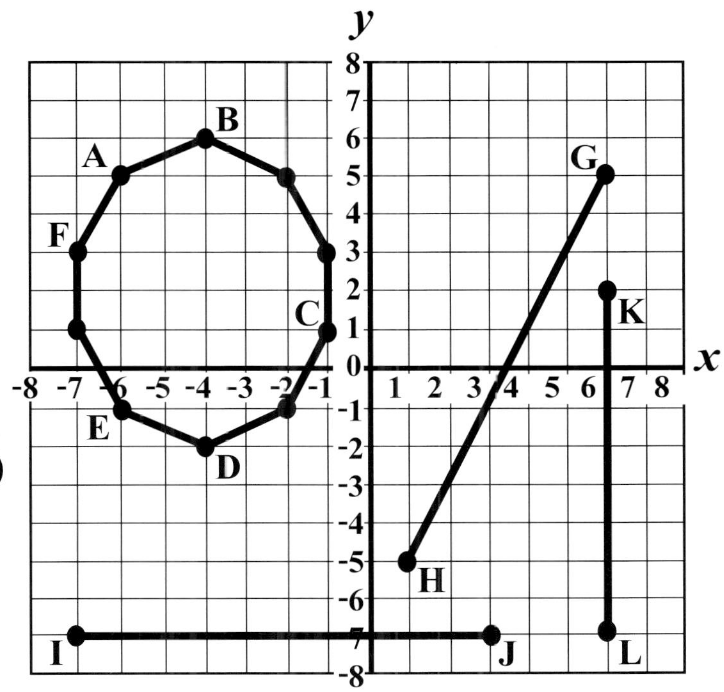

v) Lines **I/J** and **K/L** are

....

to each other.

Draw in and give the new **Coordinates**:

9a) For Shape **A** if it is **Translated 2** Squares right and **9** Squares down.

a = (   ) b = (   )

c = (   ) d = (   )

9b) For Shape **B** if it is **Reflected** in the ***x*-axis**.

a = (   ) b = (   )

c = (   )

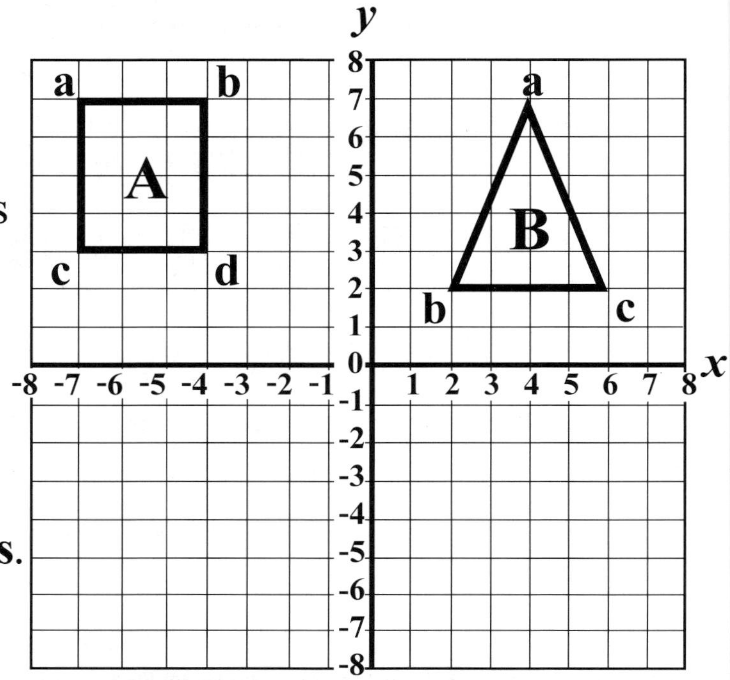

d. Logo Programs

Logo Programs enable Computers to generate Shapes or Pathways.

Example:

Guide the robot along the white Squares.

(It helps to imagine you are the robot).

Forward 3, Turn right, Forward 5, Turn left, Forward 2, Turn left, Forward 4, Turn right, Forward 4.

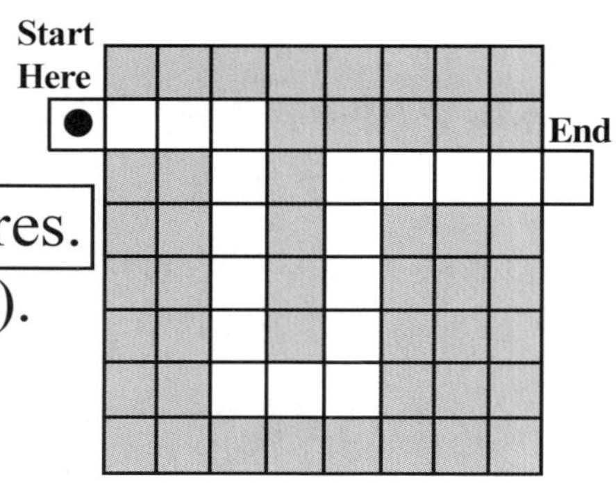

Exercise 17: 6d

10a) Direct a person through this maze.

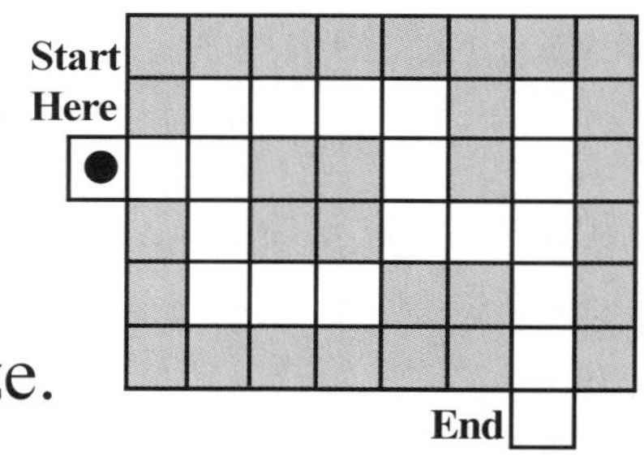

Forward 2, ...

....

....

....

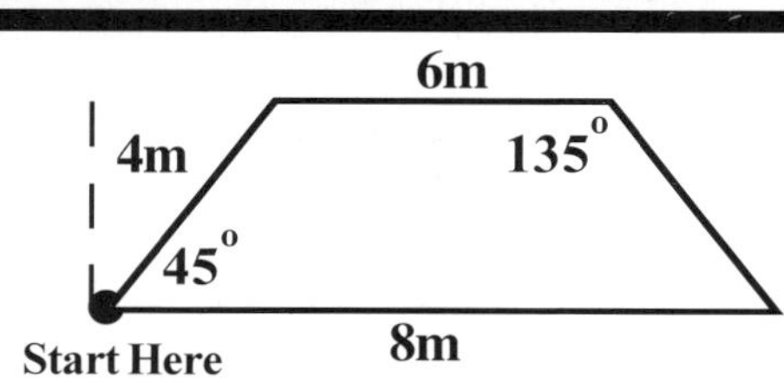

10) Write a Logo Program to draw this Trapezium.

Turn Right 45°, Forward 4m, ...

....

....

....

....

Score

Chapter Eighteen
TABLES, CHARTS, GRAPHS & DIAGRAMS
1. Statistical Data

Statistics involves the collection, display and analysis of information or Data, usually in numerical form. **Data** is the complete set of individual pieces of information that is used in any process connected with Statistics.

Data can be collected by carrying out **Surveys** using **Questionnaires**. Once a Survey is complete a Hypothesis or theory can be tested. e.g. A Survey on hair colour in your class: how many have black, brown or blonde hair?

There are four kinds of **Data**:

1. **Primary Data** - Data collected by yourself e.g. A survey conducted by yourself in your own classroom.
2. **Secondary Data** - Data that somebody else has collected. e.g. a population census.
3. **Discrete Data** - Data made up of certain definite values. e.g. A survey of shoe sizes that your class wears. This is Discrete Data because there are only a limited amount of values for the sizes in which shoes are made and sold.
4. **Continuous Data** - Data that can take any value within certain restrictions. e.g. A survey of foot lengths in your class. This is Continuous Data because feet can be of many and various lengths.

This Statistical Data is presented using **Tables**, **Charts**, **Graphs** and **Diagrams** for easy understanding and analysis.

2. Tables

a. Two-Way Tables

These can be used to calculate Probabilities **(See Book 4)**.

b. Data/Information Tables

Data can be presented in the form of Tables or Lists. They include menus, price lists, timetables, scoring sheets etc.

Example: The Prices of Fairground Rides.

Rides	Child (12 and under)	Adult
Waltzer	70p	£1.00
Ghost House	50p	75p
Watersplash	£1.00	£1.40
Roller Coaster	£1.50	£2.25

How much will it cost Mrs Porter and her two children (one is 13 years old) to take all the rides; except her 10 year old daughter who does not ride the Watersplash?

Add the adult prices - £5.40 (Double for 2 adults) **£10.80**

Add the child prices (less £1.00 - No Watersplash) **£2.70**

Total is **£13.50**

Exercise 18: 1a Answer the following:

1) This Table shows the results of the school football team over a three year period.

Year	Won	Lost	Drawn
1998	8	3	4
1999	4	9	6
2000	3	8	7

a) How many matches did they win altogether? ....

b) How many matches did they not win? ....

2) A school list holds emergency contact numbers for Asthmatic children.

Name	Class	Contact	Tel. No.
John Allen	4	Mother	458908
Lisa Peel	2	Father	618899
Nadia Sidhu	3	Aunt	219901
Elise Jones	6	Neighbour	654300
Rohit Paddan	4	Grandma	219901

a) How many children have parent contact numbers? ....

b) Which two children are related? (look for the clue).

....

c) Which class has to be watched more carefully? ....

c. Distance Tables

This Table is in kilometres

Chorley				
8	Pemble			
15	12	Apley		
22	19	15	Milton	
33	41	20	17	Tindall

A Distance Table shows Distances in Miles or Kilometres between different places.

Example:

What is the Distance between Chorley and Milton?

(Follow the arrows to see how the Distance is found).

The Distance is **22 kilometres**.

Exercise 18: 1b

Answer the following:

3) From the Air Miles Table state the Distances:

London				
330	Paris			
300	400	The Hague		
420	310	250	Brussels	
600	620	400	430	Hamburg

a) London to Paris .... miles.

b) Paris to Hamburg .... miles.

c) The Hague to Brussels .... miles.

d) If a London businessman flew there and back to all these cities one at a time, the total Distance covered would be .... miles.

d. Tabular Questions

Some questions can be answered by creating a Table.
Example:

Paul and Joseph like tennis; Leah and Marsha do not. Marsha and Joseph like Swimming; the others like ten-pin bowling. Paul likes soccer; the others do not.

a) What is the least popular sport? b) Who likes most sports?

c) How many people like swimming but do not like bowling?

The Table gives the answers.
a) **Soccer** b) **Paul**
c) **2 people.**

Child	Tennis	Swimming	Bowling	Soccer
Paul	Yes	No	Yes	Yes
Joseph	Yes	Yes	No	No
Leah	No	No	Yes	No
Marsha	No	Yes	No	No

Exercise 18: 1c Answer the following:

4) There are five girls called Anne, Betty, Carol, Delia and Ellen. Anne, Carol and Delia have brown hair and the others have fair hair. Betty, Carol and Ellen have blue eyes. Betty and Ellen are friends. Anne and Ellen are tall.

(Abbreviation e.g. **T** stands for **Tall**)

	B/H	F/H	B/E	F	T
A					
B					
C					
D					
E					

a) How many girls have blue eyes and have friends in the group? .... girls.
b) Which girl has no friends in the group and is tall? ....
c) How many girls have brown hair, blue eyes and are not tall? .... girl(s).
d) Which girls do not have blue eyes but have have brown hair? .... and ....

---

5) A, B, C, D, E and F are six cities. Cities A, C and F have a theatre. B, D and F have cathedrals and rivers, C only has a river. Only Cities B and C have no factories.

a) Which city has no theatre or river? City ....
b) How many cities have theatres and factories? .... cities.
c) City .... has a theatre, a cathedral and factories.

e. Tally (Frequency or Distribution) Tables

Tallying is an easy way of Counting an event each time it occurs. Example: Counting goals in a game of football.

Up to 4 are Counted as vertical strokes. |||| = 4

5 is made by striking a diagonal line across the 4 strokes. 𝍸 = 5

Discrete data can be recorded on a Tally (Frequency) Table.

Example:

25 pupils in Year 5 were given a mental arithmetic test. The Data shows their marks out of 10.
9, 4, 6, 9, 8, 9, 4, 6, 9, 8, 5, 9, 9, 8, 4, 4, 9, 8, 6, 4, 8, 4, 7, 7, 9

Mark	Tally	Frequency
4	𝍸 |	**6**
5	|	**1**
6	|||	**3**
7	||	**2**
8	𝍸	**5**
9	𝍸 |||	**8**

The mark Frequency is recorded e.g. **4 marks** occurs **6 times**.

Exercise 18: 1d Answer the following:

6) Find the Frequency of the 5 vowels in this passage from a Shakespeare play.

'All the world's a stage,
and all the men and women merely players;
They have their exits and their entrances;
And one man in his time plays many parts.
His acts being seven ages. At first the infant,
Mewling and puking in the nurse's arms.
And then the whining school-boy, with his satchel,
And shining morning face, creeping like snail
Unwillingly to school.' (From 'As You Like It')

Letter	Tally	Fr
a	𝍸 𝍸 𝍸 𝍸 𝍸 |	26
e		
i		
o		
u		

f. Grouped Data and Class Intervals

Data can be arranged into Groupings or Classes. Example:

Arrange the same 25 maths pupils into low (4-5 marks), middle (6-7 marks) and top (8-9 marks) Group.

Marks	Tally	Frequency
4-5	𝍸 ||	**7**
6-7	𝍸	**5**
8-9	𝍸 𝍸 |||	**13**

The Class Interval is the full extent of a Grouping. Here it is 2 marks.

Exercise 18: 1e Answer the following:

7) This is a Survey of school journey Times for a year 5 class (recorded in minutes). Using a Class Interval of **15 minutes**, complete the Table.

8, 9, 14, 35, 12, 10, 17, 27, 30, 50, 12, 45, 59, 43, 14, 52, 43, 25, 31, 41, 6, 9, 18, 37, 49, 12, 53, 38, 31, 45

Times	Tally	Fr
1-15	卌 卌	10

Remember: $>$ means 'greater than' $<$ means 'less than'

The hungry mouth $<$ always swallows the bigger amount. e.g. $4 < 10$, $10 > 4$

Class Intervals can be written using **Inequality Signs.**

Example: Write the Value (*v*) 'greater than or equal to' **25** but 'less than' **50.**

It is written as: $\mathbf{25 \leq v < 50}$

It basically means **the Value is between 25 and 50.**

1. The Symbol $\leq$ means (*v*) is equal to or greater than 25.
2. The Symbol $<$ means (*v*) must be less than 50.

These two additional signs have to be understood and learnt.

To summarise, the Symbols are as follows:
$\geq$ means 'greater than or equal to'
$\leq$ means 'less than or equal to'

These Signs can then be used in writing Frequency Tables.

Example:

20 family members attended a birthday party at a social club. A Survey of their ages was carried out.

4, 5, 9, 65, 18, 22, 37, 71, 66, 12, 19, 44, 53, 66, 73, 32, 98, 2, 7, 40

Ages	Tally	Fr
$0 < A \leq 20$	卌 |||	8
$20 < A \leq 40$	||||	4
$40 < A \leq 60$	||	2
$60 < A \leq 80$	卌	5
$80 < A \leq 100$			1

0 - 20 years is shown as (*A* is age)

'Ages greater than 0, but less than or equal to 20' $\mathbf{0 < A \leq 20}$

Exercise 18: 1f   Answer the following:

8) A railway company recorded the delays in its trains for one day (in minutes). Work out the Frequencies.

7, 19, ~~3~~, 14, ~~2~~, ~~1~~, 7, 17, 8, 16, 5, ~~3~~, 9, 10, 12, 6, 8, 11, 9, ~~4~~, 9, 17

Times (t)	Tally	Fr
$0 \le t < 5$	卌	5
$5 \le t < 10$		
$10 \le t < 15$		
$15 \le t < 20$		

---

9) The weights of all the boys in year 6 were recorded. This continuous Data ranged from **35kg to 60kg** (Each Grouping spans **5kg**). Fill in the class Intervals and the Frequencies.

~~36~~, 59, 43, 52, ~~39~~, 49, ~~38~~, ~~37~~, 51, 40, 55, 56, ~~38~~, 40, ~~36~~, 48, 41, ~~38~~, 55, 44, ~~39~~, 44, 44, 57, 44, ~~38~~, 47, 55, 50, 43

Note - The first Interval is 'greater than or equal to 35 but less than 40'

Weight (w)	Tally	Fr
$35 \le w < 40$	卌 ||||	9

g. Finding Averages from Frequency Tables

Example: See **Book 2** for Averages.

30 children cycle to school on one day. Give the **Mode**, **Mean**, **Median** and **Range** of their journey times. (The fastest journey was 1 minute and the slowest 25 minutes).

Minutes	Mid Value	Frequency (Journeys)	Mid-Value ×Frequency
1 - 5	3	5	15
6 - 10	8	4	32
11 - 15	13	2	26
16 - 20	18	10	180
21 - 25	23	9	207
Totals		**30**	**460**

For the **Modal Class:** (Group with most Frequent journey Time). - **<u>16 - 20 minutes</u>**.

For the **Mean:** (Average journey Time). Add the total Time taken in all journeys and Divide by the number of journeys. **460 ÷ 30** = **<u>15 minutes</u>** (to the nearest minute).

For the **Median:** (Middle Frequency) Count down the Frequencies to where the middle journey would be. 30 journeys were made, so count down and take the mid-value of the fifteenth and sixteenth journeys - **<u>18 minutes</u>**.

For the **Range:** (difference between the highest and lowest Value). Subtract the lowest Value from the highest Value. **25 − 1** = **<u>24</u>**.

Example:

Paul recorded the Distances his classmates had to travel to school in order to find the Mean, Median, Mode and Range.

The Frequency Table shows the number of children that travelled Distances from one to five miles.

Number of Miles Travelled	1	2	3	4	5
Frequency (number of children)	10	5	6	3	2

The Mean

$$\textbf{Mean} = \frac{\textbf{Total of the Results when Multiplied}}{\textbf{Total of the Frequency}}$$

$$= \frac{(10 \times 1) + (5 \times 2) + (6 \times 3) + (3 \times 4) + (2 \times 5)}{\textbf{Total of the Frequency}}$$

$$= \frac{10 + 10 + 18 + 12 + 10}{26} = \frac{60}{26} = \textbf{2.3 miles} \text{ (1 d.p.)}$$

The Mode, Median and Range

The **Mode** is the value that has the highest Frequency; the **Median** is the middle value and the **Range** is the difference between the lowest and the highest value.

The **Range** is **5 − 1** = **4 Miles**

The **Mode** is **1 Mile** (with a Frequency of 10.)

Number of Miles Travelled	1	2	3	4	5
Frequency (number of children)	10	5	6	3	2

The middle is between the 13th and 14th child and is in here. The **Median** is **2 Miles**.

Exercise 18: 1g Answer the following:

10) a) The number of pets that each child in a year 5 class has is classified as Discrete data. It is recorded in the Table below:

Number of Pets	0	1	2	3	4	5	6
Frequency (number of children)	3	9	3	4	4	2	1

Calculate the Mean number of pets the children have. ....

What is the Median number of pets? .... (Give your answer to 2 d.p.)

Number of children at each table.	Frequency (Number of tables)	Total number of children for table sittings.
1	3	$1 \times 3 = 3$
2	5	
3	5	
4	3	
5	4	
Totals		

Score ☐

b) Sixty Year 6 children sat at dinner tables. Fill in the Table and Add to get the totals. Then find the Mean and Range for the number of children at each table.

Mean .... Range ....

3. Charts

a. Bar Charts

Bar (Column/Block) Charts can display Frequency Data.

Example:

30 girls sat a maths exam (Marks out of 100). How many girls Scored between **61** and **80** marks?

Marks	Tally	Fr
$0 < A \leq 20$	𝍸	5
$20 < A \leq 40$	||||	4
$40 < A \leq 60$	𝍸 ||	7
$60 < A \leq 80$	𝍸 𝍸	10
$80 < A \leq 100$	||||	4

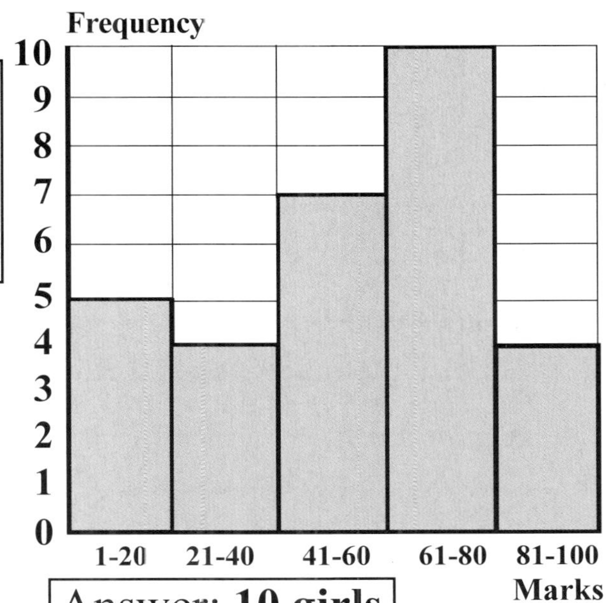

Answer: **10 girls**

The same Bar Chart can be drawn in a number of ways. Sometimes they are called **Histograms**.

Vertical Lines

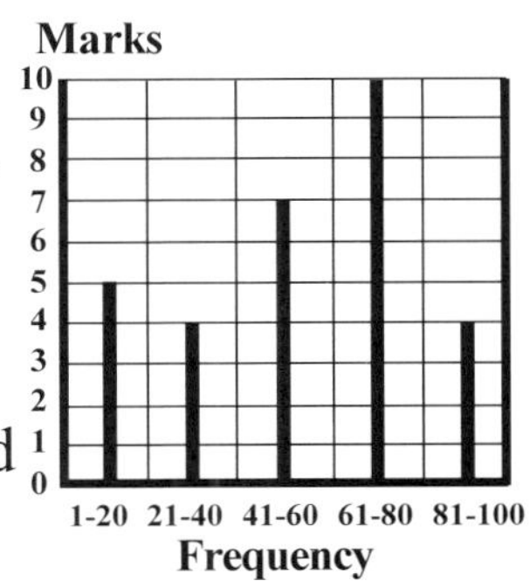

Symbols/Pictures

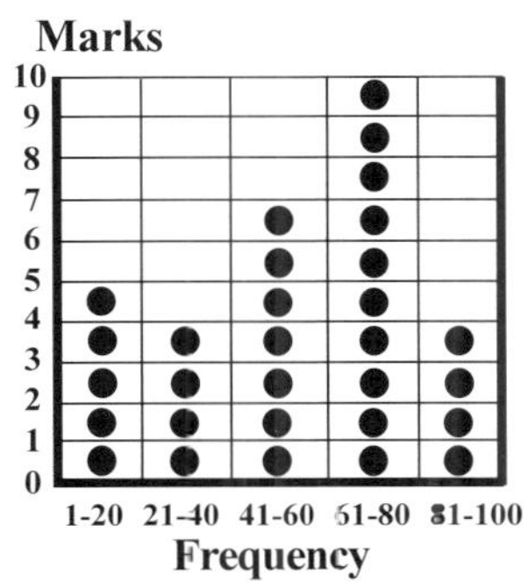

Drawn Sideways

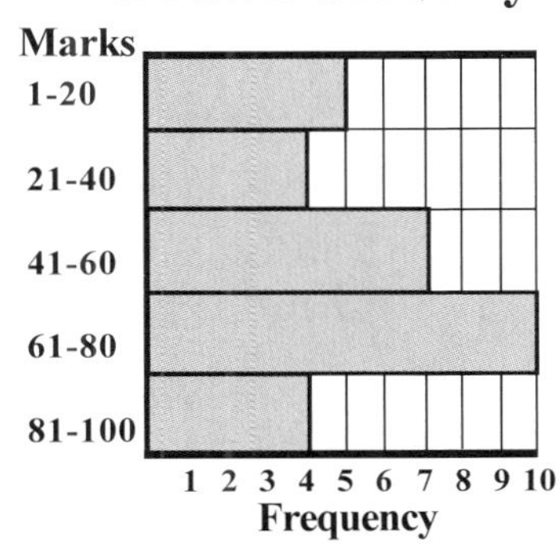

Exercise 18: 2a Answer the following:

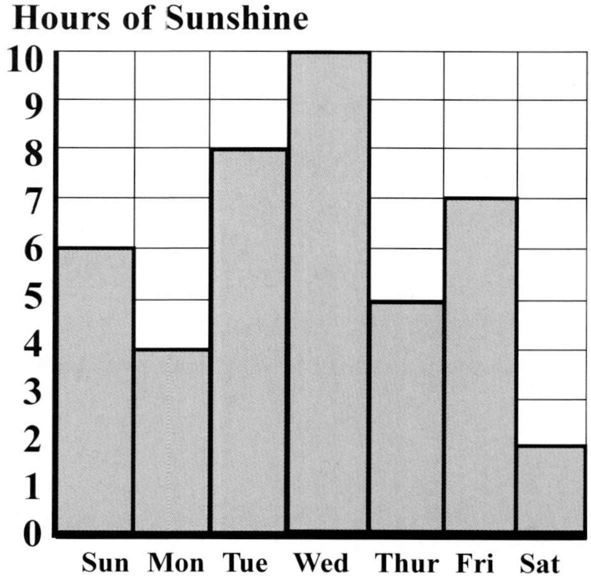

1) This Chart indicates the sunshine hours in one week.

a) Which day was the sunniest?
....

b) What was the difference in hours of sunshine between the sunniest and the least sunniest day?
.... hours.

c) What was the total hours of sunshine for the whole week?
.... hours.

d) What was the Mean number of hours of sunshine per day?
.... hours.

2) Ten teams of children competed on sports day. Draw in the Bars to show each team's performance.

Team	P/S	Team	P/S
A	**7**	F	**9**
B	**2**	G	**4**
C	**1**	H	**10**
D	**5**	I	**3**
E	**2**	J	**8**

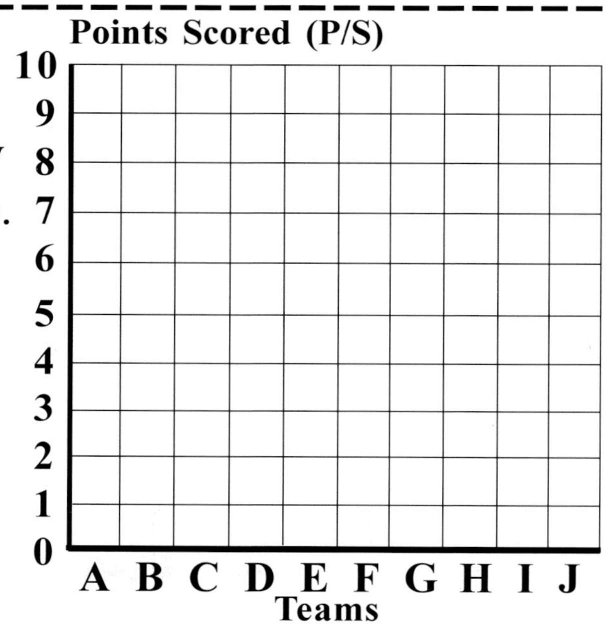

3) The Bar Chart shows the heights of a class of children. This is Continuous data.

a) How many children are at least **135cm** tall but less than **150cm**?
.... children.

b) How many children are under **140cm**? .... children.

c) There are ten children with a height of greater than **145cm**. True or false? ....

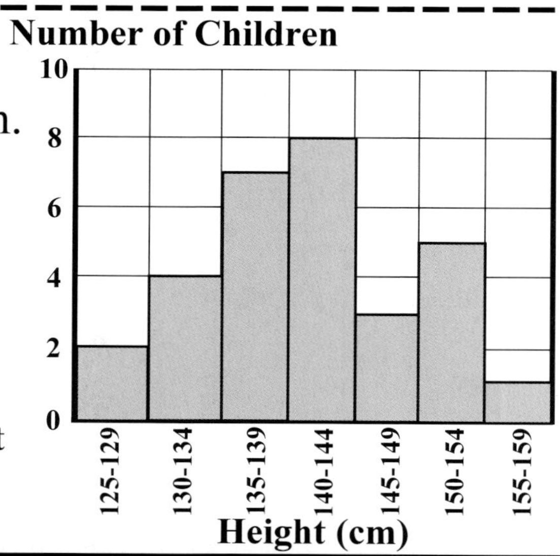

b. Pie Charts

Pie Charts show things as parts of a whole.
Each sector can be Calculated in Fractions, Degrees or Percentages.
Example:

Philip Shares his birthday cake with **4** friends. Mandy takes her Share first. What is the size of Mandy's share?

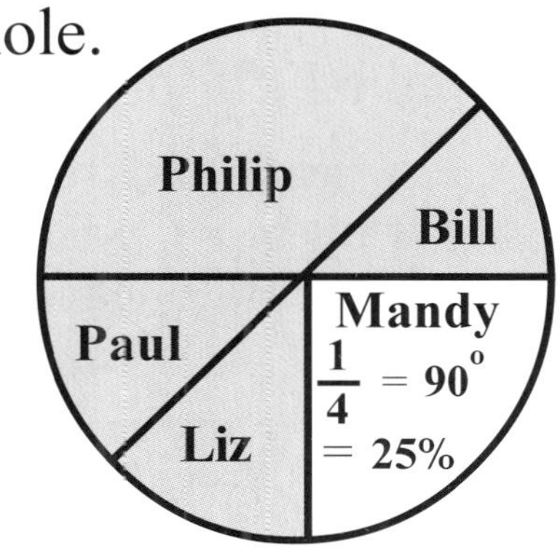

Answer: Mandy's Share is $= \frac{1}{4} =$ **25%** $=$ **90°**

For Conversion techniques of the above see the following:

See Book 3 - Percentages/Fractions **See Book 4 - Angles/Fractions**

Fractions and Percentages are often easily recognisable.

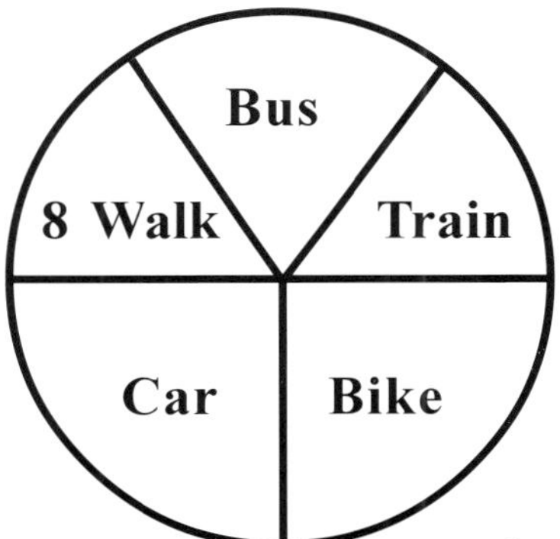

Example:

A Survey was carried out in Year 5 and 6 to find out what types of transport children used to come to school. If **8** children walk, find the Missing Amounts on the Pie Chart.

We can see that $\frac{1}{6}$ of the Chart represents the **8** children that walk. (Half the Chart represents **3** $\times$ **8** $=$ **24** children).

Therefore: $\frac{1}{6}$ = **8** by bus; $\frac{1}{6}$ = **8** by train; $\frac{1}{4}$ = **12** by car; $\frac{1}{4}$ = **12** by bike. The Pie Chart represents **48** children.

Exercise 18: 2b Answer the following:

4) A group of children were Surveyed about their favourite colours. How many children liked:

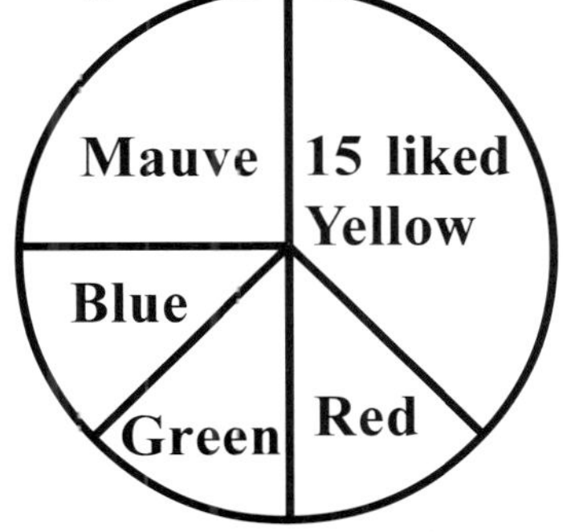

a) Red? .... b) Green? ....

c) Blue? .... d) Mauve? ....

e) The total number of children asked was ....

5) A Survey of favourite types of TV programme was conducted among the **64** children in Year 5.

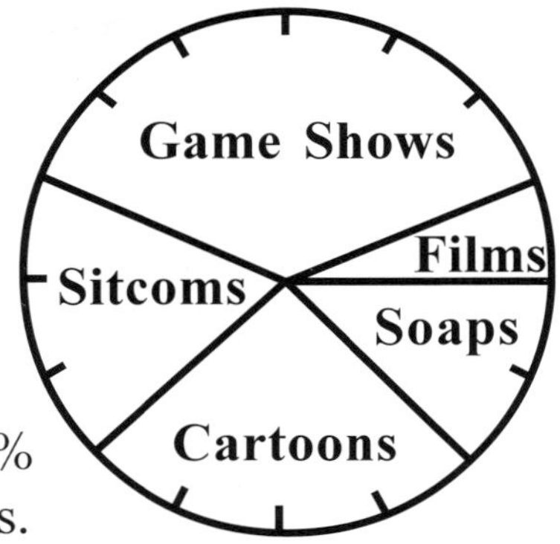

a) What Fraction of children liked Cartoons? ....
b) How many children liked Sitcoms? ....
c) What Percentage of children liked Soaps? ....%
d) Game Shows are represented by .... degrees.

---

6) Year 6 conducted a Survey that Counted the number of vehicles passing their school in a **3 hour** period.

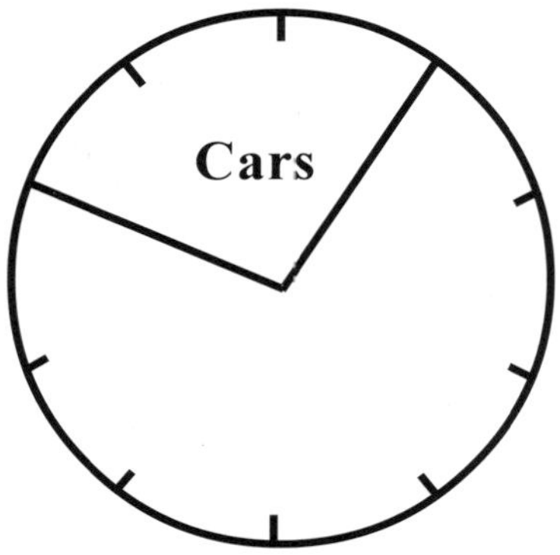

Buses = **10%**; Lorries = $\frac{1}{5}$; Vans = $\frac{1}{10}$
Motor Bikes = **18**; Bicycles = **36°**

Fill in the information on the Chart.

7) Now answer the following:

a) How many cars were Counted? ....
b) What was the total vehicle Count? ....
c) Calculate the Average (Mean) number of vehicles per hour ....

Relating Angles to numbers of other things:

Example: A Frequency Table shows how Sam spends his day. Draw a Pie Chart to represent the Table.

1. Find one hour in Degrees. 2. Multiply by the Frequency.

e.g. 1 hr in Degrees $= \frac{360}{24} = \mathbf{15^o}$; So sleep $= 9 \times 15 = \mathbf{135^o}$

or $\frac{9}{24} \times 360 = \mathbf{135^o}$

Activity	Fr. (hrs)	Angle
Sleep	9	135°
Meals	2	30°
School	7	105°
TV	3	45°
Clubs	2	30°
Travel	1	15°
Total	**24**	**360°**

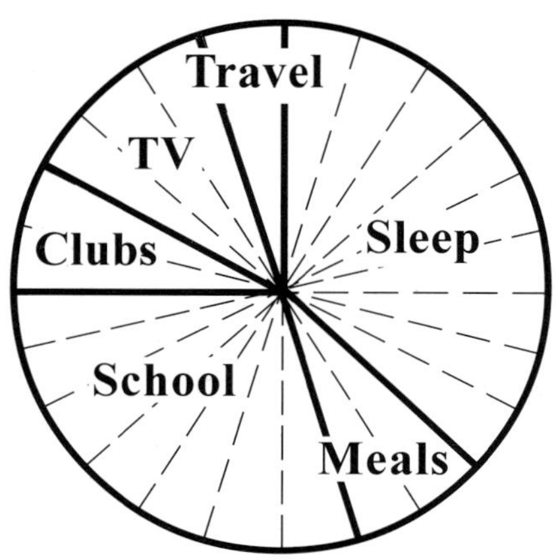

Exercise 18: 2c Answer the following: **Score** [ ]

8) A Survey of **30** children Recorded their favourite pets.
Calculate the Angles for each Sector.

Rabbit $= \frac{12}{30} \times 360 = 144^o$ or

Each Choice $= \frac{360}{30} = 12^o$

Rabbit $= 12 \times 12 = 144^o$

Pet	**Fr.**	**Angle**
Rabbit	**12**	**144°**
Cat	**4**	
Dog	**2**	
Hamster	**9**	
Budgie	**3**	
Total	**30**	

9) Draw the Chart.

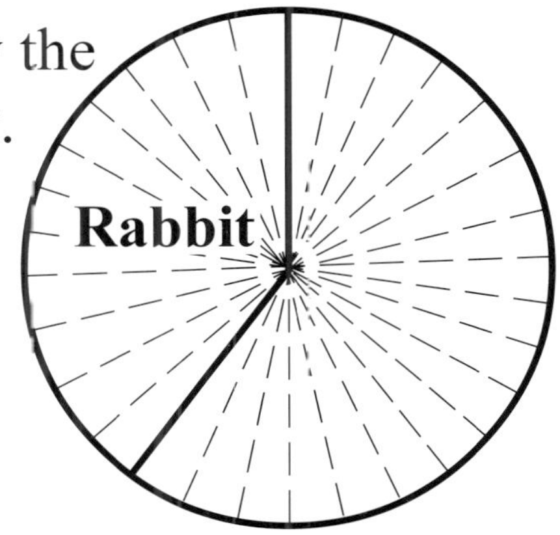

---

10) **20** children voted to appoint a youth club chairman from **3** candidates.
Complete the Table and Chart.

Candidate	**Fr. (Votes)**	**Angle**
Jonathan	**8**	
Jaspreet	**5**	
Paula	**7**	
Total	**20**	

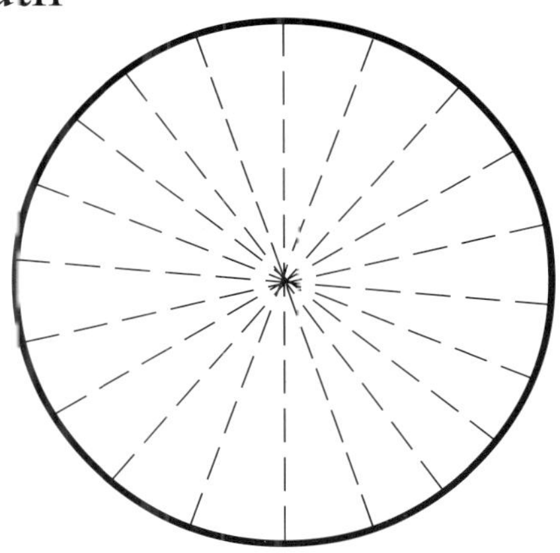

4. Graphs

a. Line Graphs

A Line Graph is similar to a Bar Chart. Points are Plotted in the middle of the Class Intervals (see circles). If straight lines are used between points it is also called a **Frequency Polygon**.

Example:

Redraw this Bar Chart as a Line Graph.

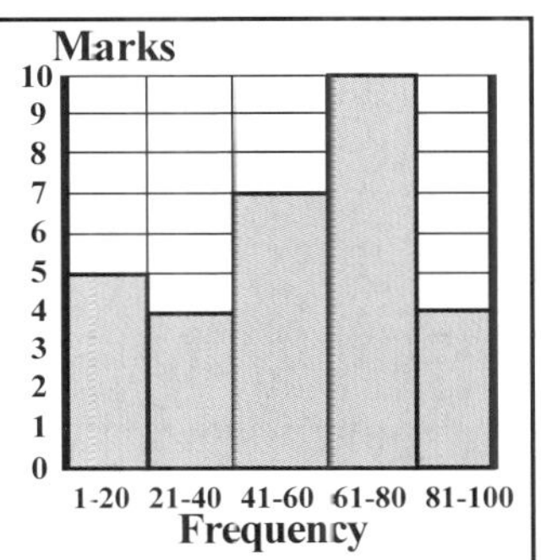

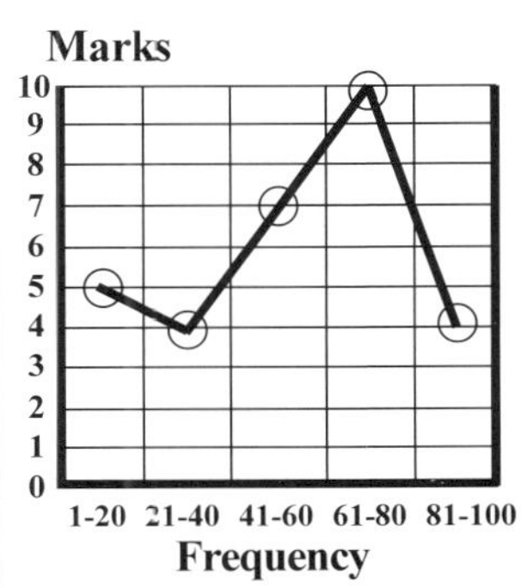

Exercise 18: 3a

Answer the following:

1) Police monitored the speed of vehicles on a stretch of road.

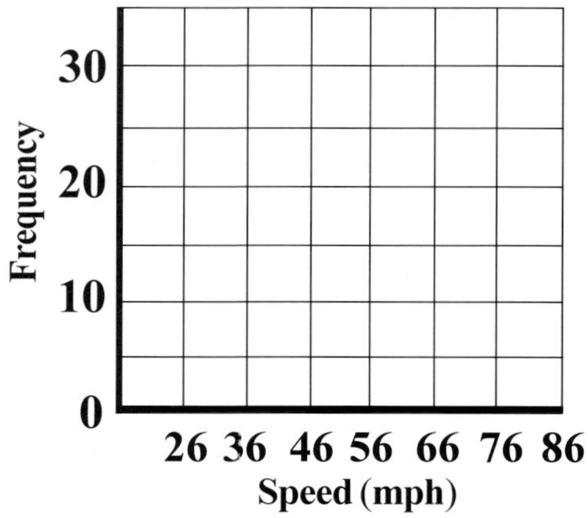

Speed	21+	31+	41+	51+	61+	71+	81+
Freq.	15	30	33	22	26	7	3

Hint: the middle of the Class Intervals are at 26, 36, ...

a) Draw a Line Graph of the information.

b) How many vehicles were checked? ....

c) If the speed limit was 50mph, how many motorists were speeding? ....

2) English and Maths results were compared in a school.

English		Maths	
Mark (%)	Fr	Mark (%)	Fr
41-50	2	41-50	0
51-60	6	51-60	1
61-70	12	61-70	8
71-80	16	71-80	16
81-90	14	81-90	20
91-100	4	91-100	14

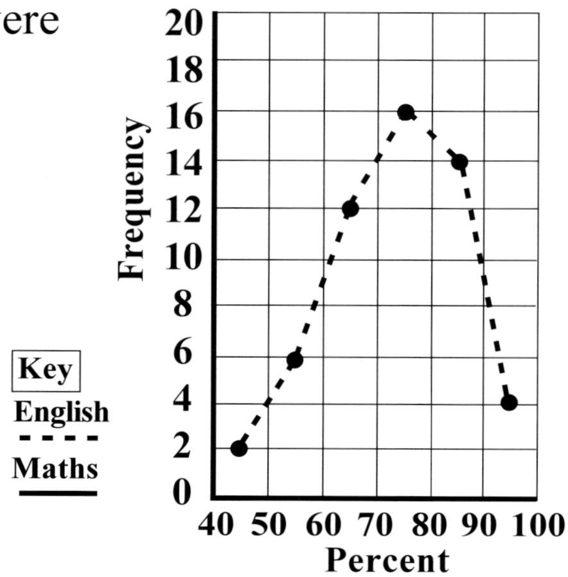

a) Plot the Points and draw the Maths Line. b) At what Percentage Interval did the same number of pupils Score the same in both subjects? ....%

c) In which subject did more children score the top mark? ....

b. Conversion Graphs

Conversion Graphs are used to Convert Measurements.

Example:

Convert **50** miles to km.

Draw a Horizontal line across to the Conversion Line and then draw a Vertical Line down.

Answer: **50 miles = 80km.**

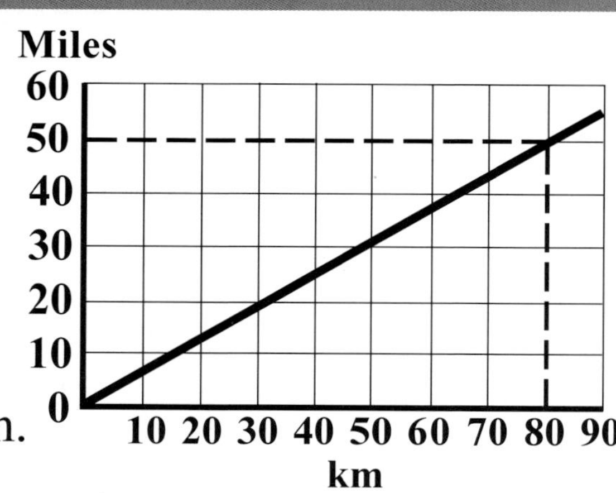

Exercise 18: 3b

Give the Approximate Conversions:

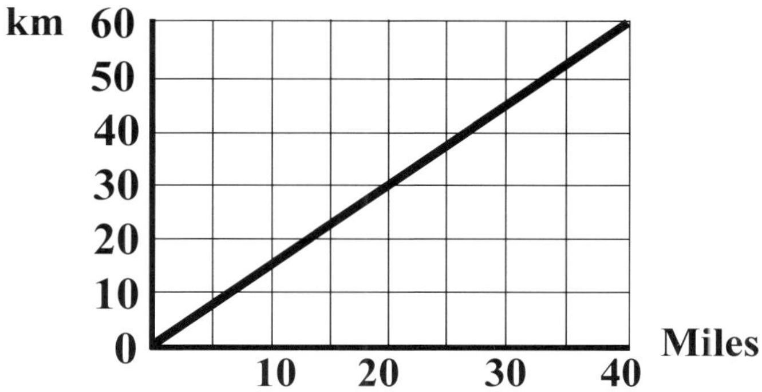

3) Miles & Kilometres

a) **60km** = ... miles.

b) **200 miles** = ... km.

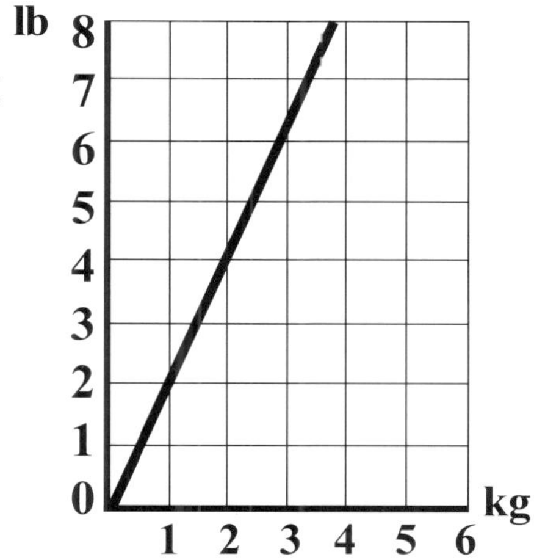

4) Pounds & Kilograms

a) **4lbs** = ... kg.

b) **3.5kg** = ... lbs.

c. *Travel Graphs*

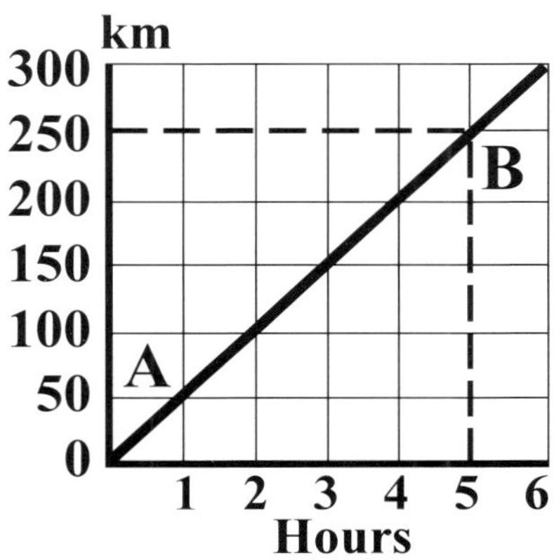

For **Time** read off axis as above = **5hrs**

Travel Graphs work the same way as Conversion Graphs. Time, Distance and Speed can be found at a glance. (See **Book 4** for Formulae)

Example:

A coach travels **250km** from A to B. What is its journey Time and Speed?

Speed = $\frac{\textbf{Distance}}{\textbf{Time}} = \frac{\textbf{250}}{\textbf{5}}$ = **50km/hr**

Exercise 18: 3c Answer the following:

5) A train travels **300 miles**.

Find the Speed for stages

a) A to B = ... mph.

b) B to C = ... mph.

c) What was the overall Distance travelled at **25mph**? .... miles.

d) Overall Average Speed from A to D = ... mph.

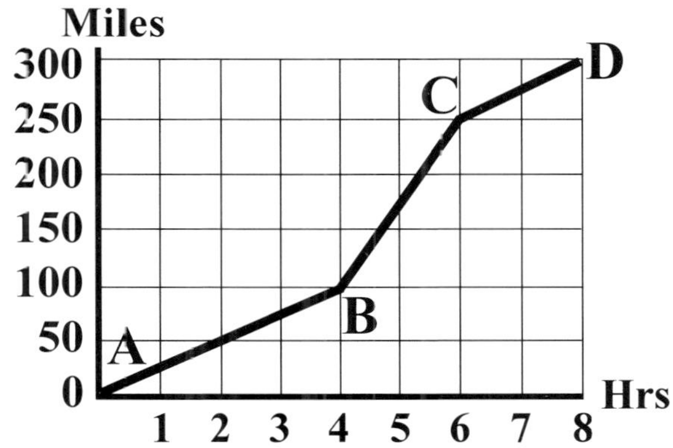

6) Rajan, Kevin and Sanjay arrange to meet at their youth club at **7.00p.m.** Rajan jogs and Kevin cycles. Sanjay catches a bus at **6.10p.m.** and arrives exactly on time. He travels **12km**.

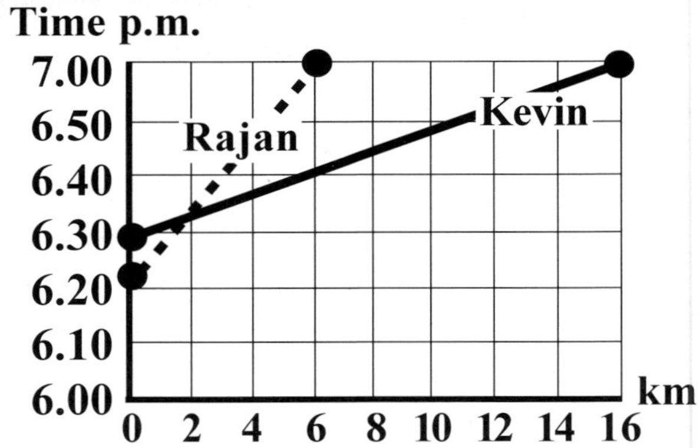

a) Draw in a Line for Sanjay. b) Whose journey is shortest? ....

c) How far does Kevin go? .... km. d) What is his Speed? .... km/hr.

e) At what Time (to the nearest 5 minutes) had Sanjay and Kevin gone the same Distance? .... p.m.

d. Scatter Graphs

A Scatter Graph represents two Measurements at once and may show whether there is a connection between them.

Example: **12** pupils complete a Level 6 test in Maths and English. Compare their marks between the two subjects on a Scatter Graph.

Name	Paul	Polly	Joan	Kirin	John	Dave	Dana	Mike	Raj	Lisa	Jack	Soni
Maths	40	60	20	30	60	75	45	80	60	35	50	70
English	40	65	25	35	60	70	50	75	70	40	55	75

Each Point is Plotted on the *x* and *y* axes. The points are Scattered about. A clear pattern shows there is **Correlation**.

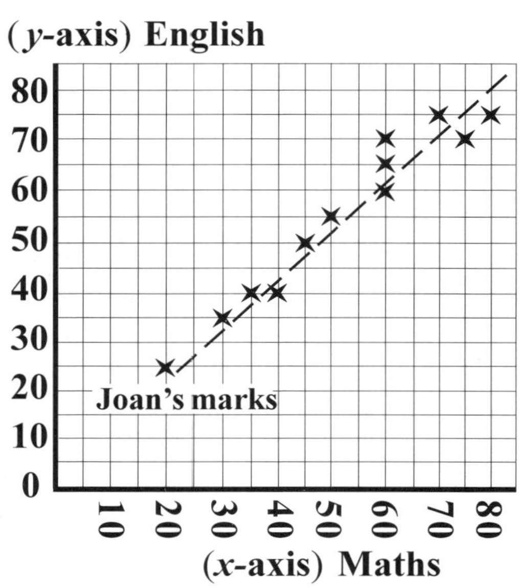

A Straight Line called **'The Line of Best Fit'** can be drawn to show the overall trend.

This is a Relationship between the two Variables. e.g. In this Group children Scoring higher in Maths also tended to Score higher in English.

This is a **Positive Correlation** because, as one Variable increases in size, so does the other one. The Plotted Points slant upwards from left to right on the Graph.

Negative Correlation

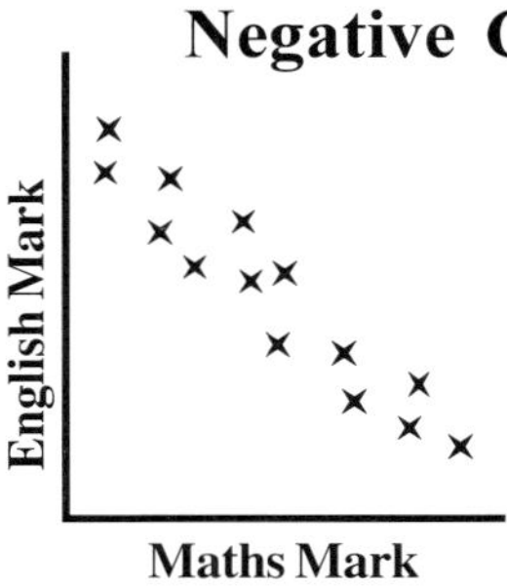

This is where one Variable decreases in size as the other increases. e.g. The English scores went down as the Maths scores went up. It slants downwards from left to right.

No Correlation

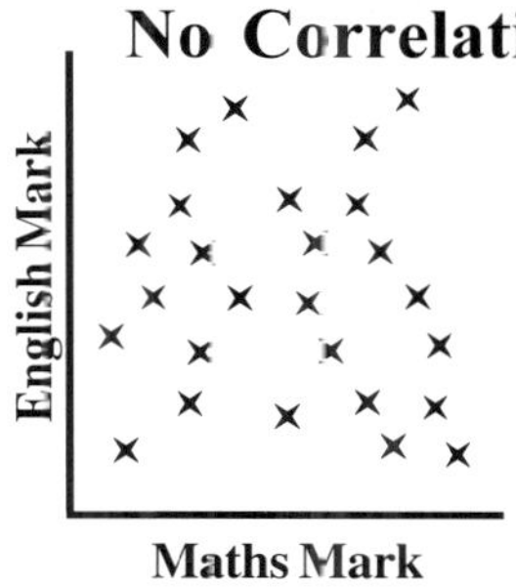

This is where there is no pattern and therefore no relationship between the Variables. e.g. Some children score low in maths but high in English and vice versa.

Correlations can also be **Weak**, **Moderate** or **Strong**. e.g. A Weak, Positive Correlation might have just enough pattern for there to be some relationship.

Exercise 18: 3d Answer the following:

Score

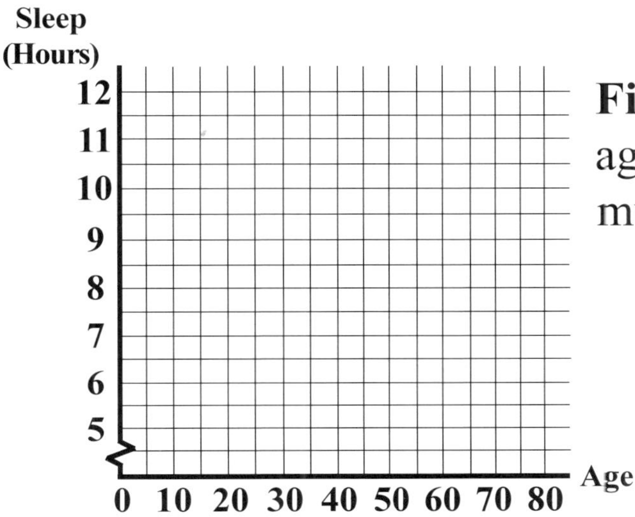

Fifteen people of various ages were Surveyed on how much sleep they needed.

7) Plot all the points on the Scatter Graph.

8) Name the kind of Correlation shown.

....

Age	5	10	15	20	25	30	35	40	45	50	55	60	65	70	75
Sleep	12	11	10.5	10	9	8	7	7	7.5	6.5	6	6	5.5	6	5.5

---

9) **Ten** children of different ages were asked how much pocket money they received.

Age	6	7	8	9	10	11	12	13	14	15
£	3	2	2	5	6	5	7	8	10	8

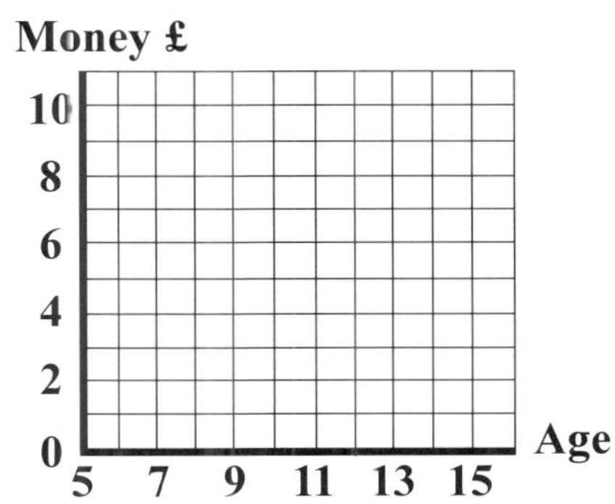

Plot the Scatter Graph. If the children are older do they usually get more? ....

---

10) Name the Correlations and state whether they are Weak, Moderate or Strong.

a)

b)

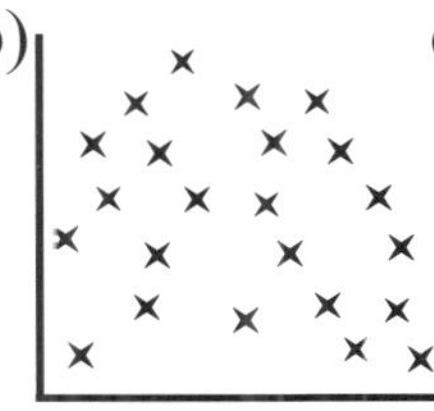

c)

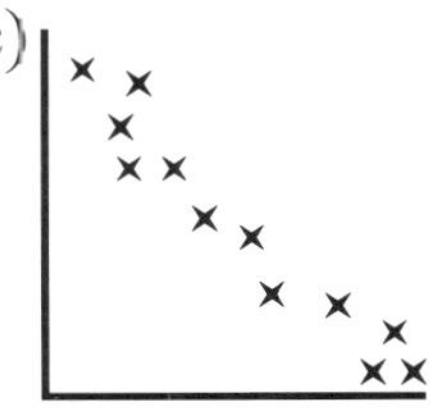

a) .... b) .... c) ....

5. Diagrams

a. Sample Space & Tree Diagrams

These Diagrams are often used to calculate Probabilities (See **Book 4**).

b. Pictograms

In Pictograms pictures represent a certain number of items.

Example: Forest School Surveyed how many children wear glasses in years 4, 5 and 6.
a) How many children wear glasses in Year 5?
b) How many children wear glasses altogether?

 stands for 6 children  stands for 3 children

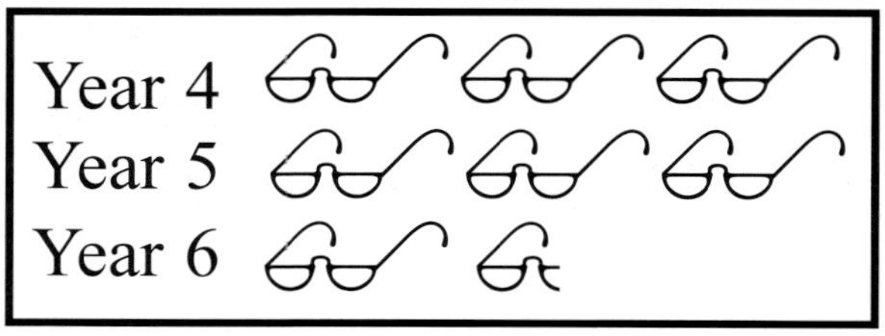

Answers:
a) **18 children** in Year 5 wear glasses.
b) **45 children** wear glasses altogether.

Exercise 18: 4a Answer the following:

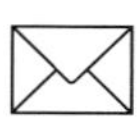 **- 10 Letters**  **- 5 Letters**

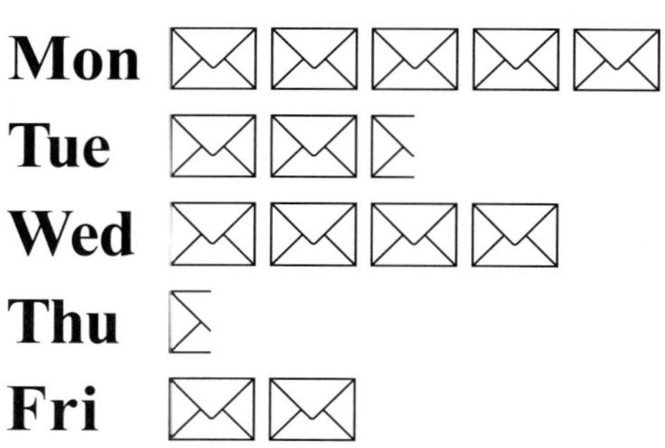

1) A business monitored the number of letters it received in one week.
a) How many letters came on Monday? ....
b) On what day was the least number of letters delivered? ....
c) What was the total number of letters for the week? ....

c. Set and Venn Diagrams

(i). Set and Venn Diagram Rules

A **Set** is a Collection of things that belong together. Things that belong to a Set are called **Members** or **Elements**.

Curly Brackets or **Braces** are drawn round a Set - { }
Commas are used to separate Members from each other.

A **Capital Letter** can stand for a Set. eg. F for fruit.

Example: **P = Prime Numbers under fifteen.**

P = { 2, 3, 5, 7, 11, 13}

The Members of a Set can be **written out in Short** or **in Full**. Also, the Members of a Set can be written out in any order.

Example: **S = Set of Seasons of the Year.**

It can be written **in short** as: **S = {Seasons}**
or in full as: **S = {Spring, Summer, Autumn, Winter}**

An **Empty Set** is a Set which contains no members. It can be called a **NULL Set** or a **VOID Set**. It can be written as:

{ } - Empty Brackets <u>**or**</u> with this Symbol Ø

Example: **R is the Set of 5 sided Rectangles.**

R = { } or R = Ø

When Sets are **Finite** their number of Members is limited.

Example: **O is the Set of Odd Numbers up to 10.**

O = { 1, 3, 5, 7, 9 }.

An **Infinite Set** is a Set which continues forever. There is no limit to the number of Members. It is ∞ or endless.

Example: **P is the Set of Prime Numbers.**

P = ∞ { 2, 3, 5, 7, 11, 13, 17 etc}.

The Number of Members of a Set is written **n** followed by the name of the Set in ordinary Brackets.

Example 1: **Show the number of Members if S is the Set of Seasons of the year.**

If **S = {Spring, Summer, Autumn, Winter}**

The number of members is **4** so: **n(S) = 4**

Example 2: **Show the number of Members if F is the Set of reptiles that fly.**

Since **F** = **{ }** **or** **F** = Ø, **n(F) = 0**

There are two Symbols that indicate whether or not a particular Element is of a specific Set.

$\in$ is a Symbol that means **'is a Member of'**

$\notin$ is a Symbol that means **'is <u>not</u> a Member of'**

Example 1: **2** is a Member of the set of Prime Numbers.

It is written **2 $\in$ {Prime Numbers}**

Example 2: **4** is **not** a Member of the Set of Prime Numbers.

It is written **4 $\notin$ {Prime Numbers}**

A **Venn Diagram** is a way of showing Sets in picture form. The contents of each Set is placed within a circular shape.

Example: Show E is the Set of eating implements using a Venn Diagram.

E = **{knife, fork, spoon}**

E

The space inside the Venn Diagram is called a **REGION**

Exercise 18: 4b

Write these Sets in short with Letters and Brackets:

2) a) **T** is the **Set of Triangles** **T** = {....................}

b) **C** is the **Set of Colours** ....

c) **P** is the **Set of Planets** ....

d) **A** is the **Set of apples made in Factories** ....

Write the List and Number of Members in these Sets:

e) **W** is the **Set of Days of the week**.

W = { .... , ... , ... ,
.... , ... , ... , ...}

The Number of Members can be written as n(......) = ...

f) **J** is the **Set of months beginning with J**.

J = { ....}

The Number of Members can be written as ....

g) **P** is the **Set of Pentagons with 3 sides**.

P = ... The Number of Members can be written as ....

h) If the Set of Even Numbers **E** = **{2, 4, 6, 8, 10 etc}** continued forever it would be an .... set.

Answer the following using the symbols $\in$ and $\notin$

i) Set **A** = **{Fruit}** Set **B** = **{Vegetables}** Set **C** = **{Meat}**

Apple .... {Fruit} Pea .... {Fruit} Lamb .... {Meat}

Pear .... {Vegetable} Beef .... {Fruit} Pork .... {Meat}

j) **Set B** is a Set of boy's names:

Set **B** = **{Roger, Bobby, David, Navraj}**

Fill in the Regions:

B

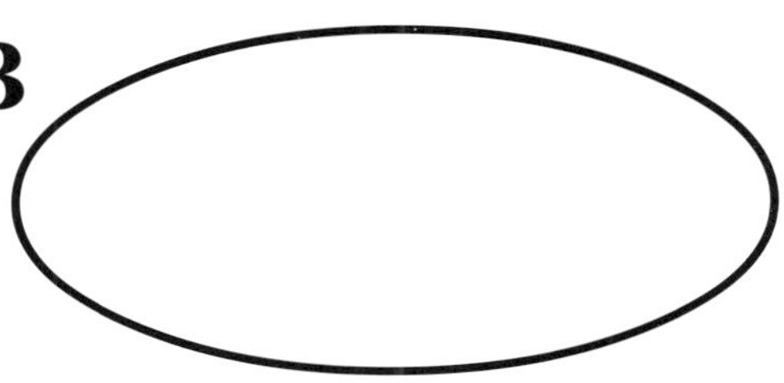

Set G is a Set of girl's names:

Set **G** = **{Emilia, Karen, Prabjit, Amy}**

Draw the Diagram:

(ii). Subsets

Subsets are smaller Sets that are also part of a Main Set.

The sign $\subset$ means 'is a **SUBSET** of'

The sign $\not\subset$ means 'is **NOT a SUBSET** of'

Example: Show how **2, 3, 4** is a Subset of **1, 2, 3, 4, 5.**

$$\{2, 3, 4\} \subset \{1, 2, 3, 4, 5\}.$$

Example: Show how **6, 7, 8** is **Not** a Subset of **1, 2, 3, 4, 5.**

$$\{6, 7, 8\} \not\subset \{1, 2, 3, 4, 5\}.$$

It is also possible to show that a **Main Set contains Subsets.**

The sign $\supset$ means '**contains** as a **Subset**'

The sign $\not\supset$ means 'does **NOT contain** as a **Subset** of'

Example: Show how **Cities** contain **London** as a Subset.

{Cities} $\supset$ **{London}**

Example: Show how **Primary Colours** does not contain **Mauve** as Subset.

{Primary Colours} $\not\supset$ **{Mauve}**

The Members of a Main Set or Subset can be Listed or Enumerated.

Example: List all the Subsets of the Set **1, 2, 3, 4, 5.**

The Subsets of **{1, 2, 3}** are:

{1, 2, 3}, **{1, 2}**, **{1, 3}**, **{2, 3}**, **{1}**, **{2}**, **{3}**, **Ø**

Note:

1. Empty Sets are Subsets of any Set. $\varnothing \subset \{1, 2, 3\}$
2. A Set is a Subset of itself. $\{1, 2, 3\} \subset \{1, 2, 3\}$
3. Set Members can be written in any order.

{1, 2, 3} is the same as {3, 2, 1}

Venn Diagram of a Subset

Example: Show the **Girls** as a **Subset** of a **Set of children.**

C = {Set of Children}

C = {Alan, Betty, Carla, Don, Elle, Fred}

G = {Betty, Carla, Elle}

The Venn Diagram shows:

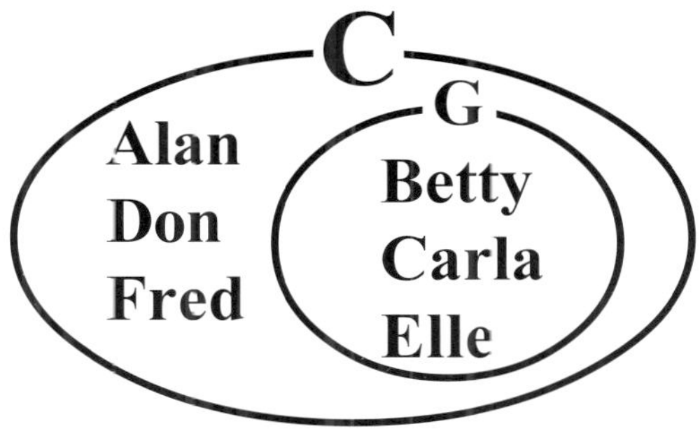

$\mathbf{G \subset C}$

G is a Subset of C

{Betty, Carla, Elle} $\subset$ {Children}

The Venn Diagram also shows:

$\mathbf{C \supset G}$ — **C contains G as a Subset**

$\mathbf{C \not\subset G}$ — **C is not a Subset of G**

$\mathbf{G \not\supset C}$ — **G does not contain C as a Subset**

Exercise 18: 4c

Answer the following:

3a) Below are a Series of Sets:

D = {2, 3, 4, 5, 6, 7, 8} Digits from 2 to 8

R = {4, 6, 8} Rectangular Numbers

T = {1, 3, 6} Triangular Numbers

N = { } Null Set

F = {1, 2, 4, 6, 8} Factors of 8

O = {9, 11, 13, 15} Odd Numbers between 8 and 16

E = {2, 4, 6, 8} Even Numbers up to 8

Define the Relationship between the Sets using Symbols

E .... F **R .... N** **T .... F** **T .... D** **R .... T**

---

b) Make a list of all the Subsets of each Set:

{Paul, Darren, Akash} {.................. , ... , ...}, {.................. , ...}, {.................. , ...}, {.................. , ...}, {..................}, {..................}, {..................}, { }

{2, 4, 6, 8} {...... , ... , ... , ...}, {...... , ... , ...}, {...... , ... , ...}, {...... , ... , ...}, {...... , ..., ...}, {...... , ...}, {...... , ...}, {...... , ...}, {...... , ...}, {...... , ...}, {...... , ...}, {......}, {......}, {......}, {......}, { }

c) Draw Venn Diagrams to show each of the following:

{18, 30} is a Subset of: **{6, 12, 18, 24, 30, 36}**

Fill in the regions:

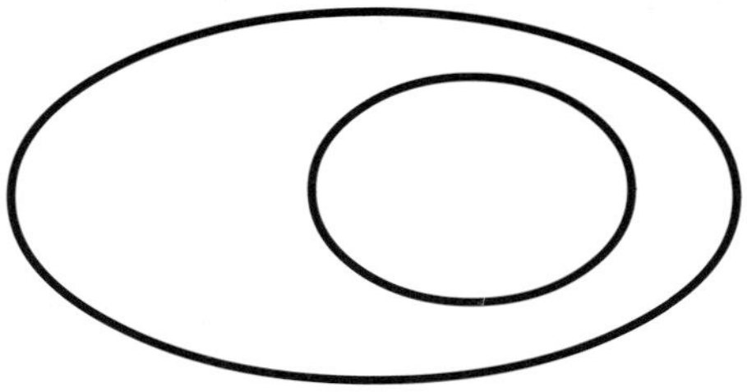

{E, F, G} is a Subset of: **{A, B, C, D, E, F, G, H, I}**

Draw the Diagram:

(iii). Intersections and Unions

When sets overlap each other it is called an **Intersection.** This is where two or more Sets have one or more Members in common. The Shared Set which contains the common Members is the **Intersection** of the original Sets.

The symbol for Intersection is $\cap$ and is called **'CAP'**.

The **Union** of two or more Sets is the Set containing all Members of these Sets.

The symbol for Union is $\cup$ and is called **'CUP'**.

Example 1:

a) Show the **Intersection** of **Girls names** and the names that begin with the letter **A**.
b) Show the **Union** of these two Sets.

Set A = **{Adam, Alan, Andrea, Andrew}**
Set G = **{Rachel, Betty, Andrea, Tina}**

The **Region** in the middle of the Sets is:

A cap G or **A** $\cap$ **G** = **{Andrea}**

The **Union** of both Sets is:

B cup A or **B** $\cup$ **A** = **{Andrew, Alan, Adam, Andrea, Rachel, Tina, Betty}**

This can be represented on a **Venn Diagram**:

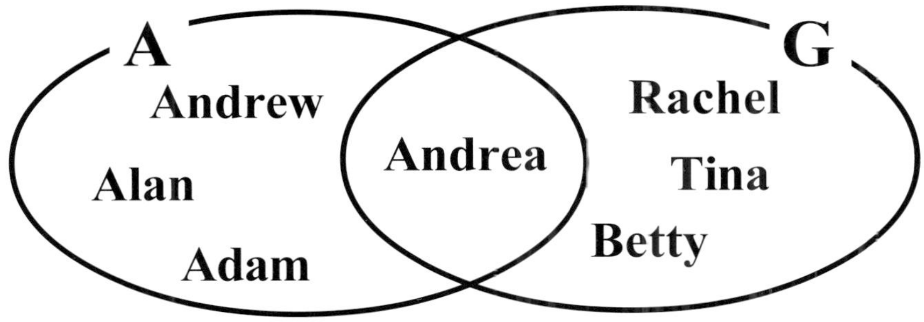

Example 2:

Show the Intersections and Union of the Sets made up from the **2×**, **3×** and **5× table** up to **30**.

Set M2 = {2, 4, 6, 8, 10, 12, 14, 16, 18, 20, 22, 24, 26, 28, 30}

Set M3 = {3, 6, 9, 12, 15, 18, 21, 24, 27, 30}

Set M5 = {5, 10, 15, 20, 25, 30}

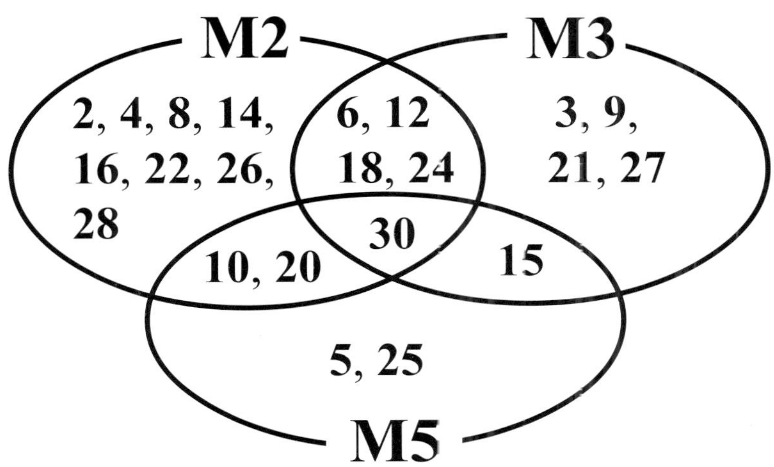

The **Intersections** of the **2×**, **3×** and **5× table** up to **30** are:

M2 ∩ M3 = {6, 12, 18, 24, 30} **M2 ∩ M5 = {10, 20, 30}**

M3 ∩ M5 = {15, 30} **M2 ∩ M3 ∩ M5 = {30}**

The **Union** of the **2×**, **3×** and **5× table** up to **30** is:

M2 cup M3 cup M5 or **M2 ∪ M3 ∪ M5** =

{2, 3, 4, 5, 6, 8, 9, 10, 12, 14, 15, 16, 18, 20, 21, 22, 24, 25, 26, 27, 28, 30}

Exercise 18: 4d Answer the following:

4a) Find the Intersection and Union of this pair of Sets and show it on the Venn Diagram below:

A = {4, 8, 12, 16, 20, 24, 28, 32, 36}, B = {1, 4, 9, 16, 25, 36}

A cap B or **A ∩ B** = {........................}

A cup B or **A ∪ B** = {...}

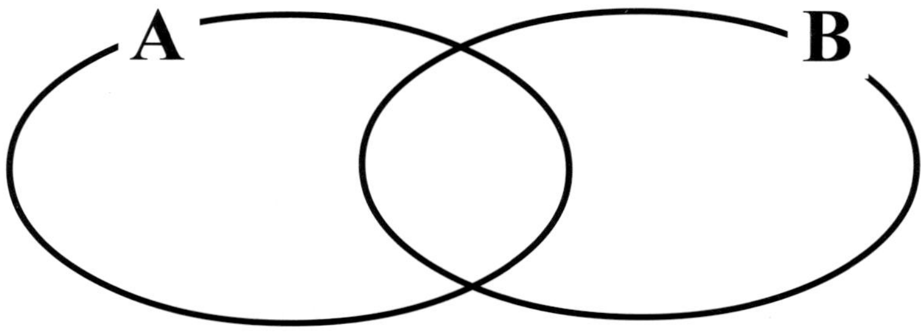

---

b) Find the Intersections and Union of these three Sets and show them on the Venn Diagram below:

A = {knight, bishop, castle, pawn}
B = {bishop, priest, vicar, dean}
C = {knight, castle, bishop, maiden, priest, chivalry}

A ∩ B = {.............} **A ∩ C** = {.............................}

B ∩ C = {...........................} **A ∩ B ∩ C** = {.............}

A ∪ B ∪ C = {...
....}

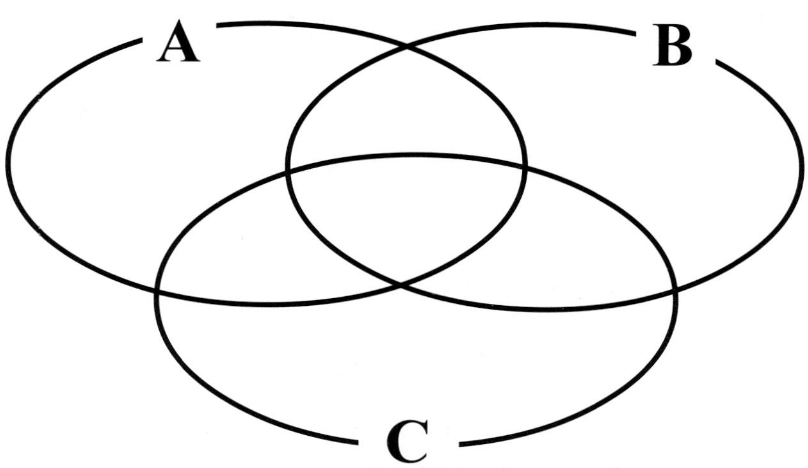

c) Find the Intersections and Union of these three Sets and draw a Venn Diagram to illustrate them:

A = **{a, e, i, o, u}** **B** = **{u, v, w, x, y, z, a, b, c, d, e}**
C = **{n, o, p, q, r, s, t, u, v, w}**

A ∩ **B** = {...............} **A** ∩ **C** = {...............}

B ∩ **C** = {...............} **A** ∩ **B** ∩ **C** = {.............}

A ∪ **B** ∪ **C** = {...}

Draw the Venn Diagram and fill in the Regions:

(iv). Additional Set Rules

Disjoint Sets are Sets that share no Members. There is no connection between them at all.

Example:

Demonstrate that **Set A** and **Set B** are Disjoint Sets.

A = **{a, b, c, d, e}** **B** = **{1, 2, 3, 4, 5}**

There are no common Members in Sets A and B so:

A = **{a, b, c, d, e}** and **B** = **{1, 2, 3, 4, 5}** are **Disjoint Sets.**

This can be shown on a Venn Diagram.

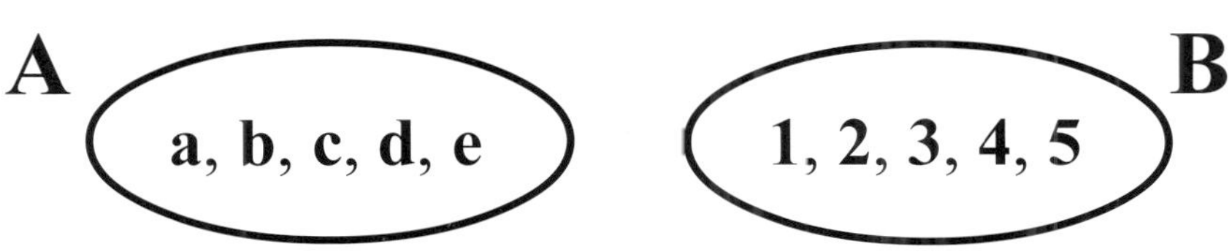

The Intersection of Disjoint Sets is always an Empty Set.

A **Universal Set** contains everything you are dealing with. All Subsets are part of the Universal Set.

A Universal Set is shown by the sign ξ

On a Venn Diagram it is shown as a rectangle.

Example: What is the Universal Set of numbers shown in the Venn diagram?

R = {6, 8, 10, 12, 14, 15, 16, 18, 20}   T = {1, 3, 6, 10, 15, 21}

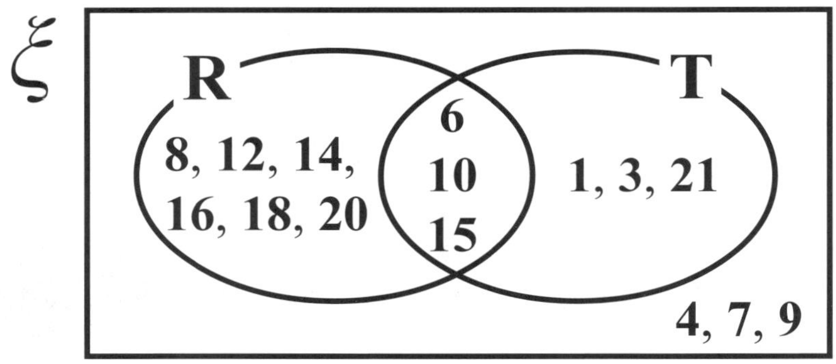

ξ **= {1, 3, 4, 6, 7, 8, 9, 10, 12, 14, 15, 16, 18, 20, 21}**

The **Complement of a Set** is all those Members which are **NOT** in that Set, but are in the original Universal Set.

Example:

What is the **Complement of Set** A?

The **Complement of Set A is denoted as A'**

ξ **= {1, 2, 3, 4, 5, 6, 7, 8, 9, 10, 11, 12}**

A = {2, 4, 6, 8, 10, 12}   B = {3, 6, 9, 12}

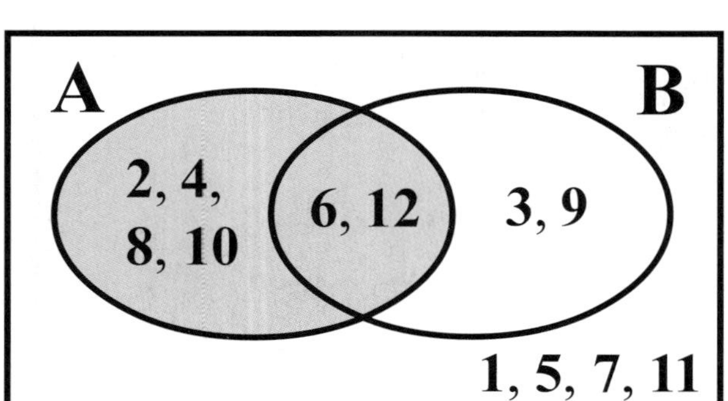

Set A is shown in grey
The Complement of Set A is everything else

Set A' = {1, 3, 5, 7, 9, 11}

(v). Sets and Carroll Diagrams

A Carroll Diagram, although seen less frequently, is an alternative way of sorting things into various Groups or Sets. It is named after the famous Children's author Lewis Carroll who wrote 'Alice in Wonderland'.

Example: Sort eight different Shapes into four basic Sets using the most obvious criteria of grouping.

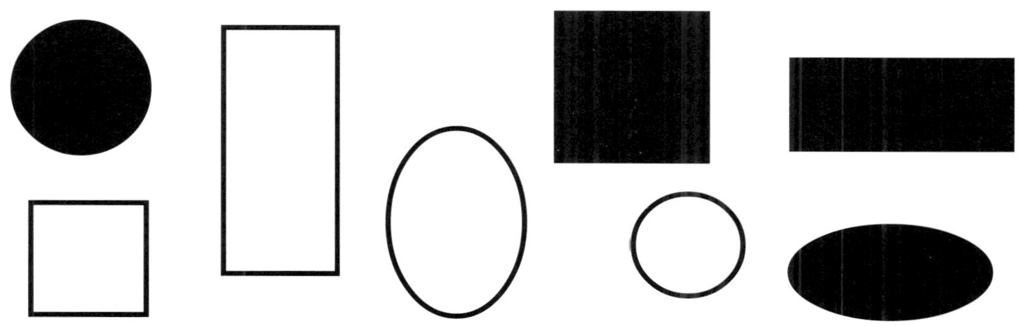

The basic Groupings would obviously be black/white and Circular/Rectangular and can be shown as follows:

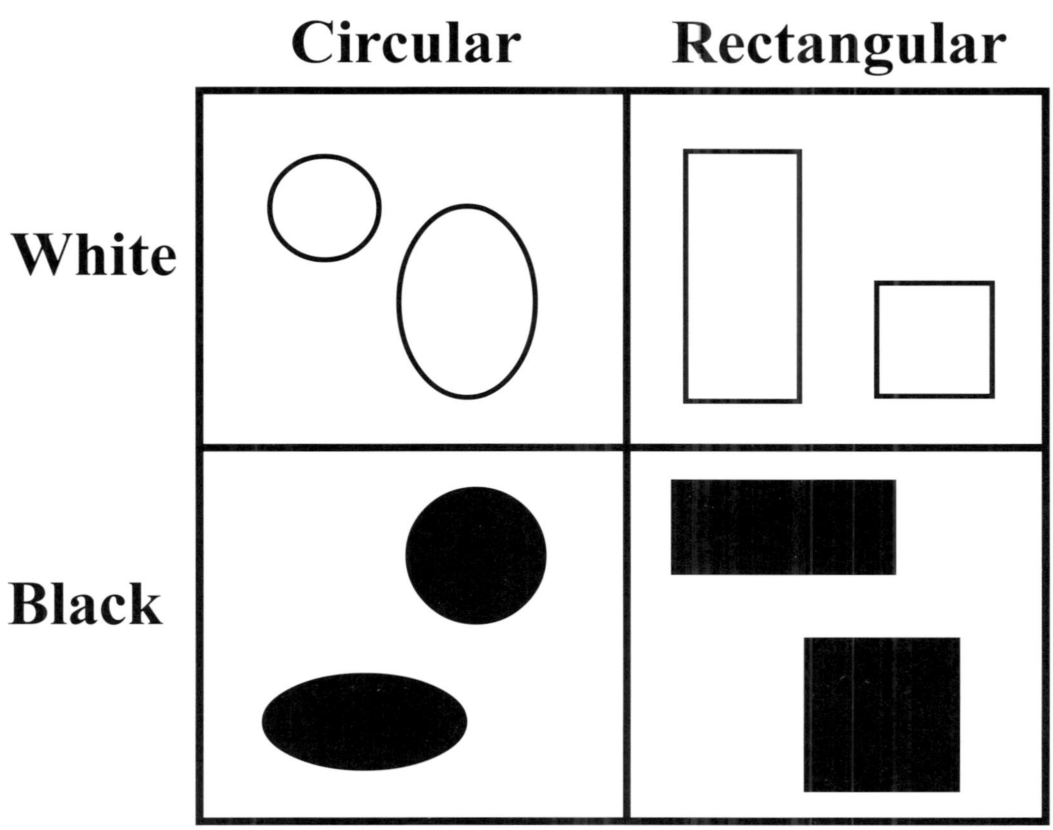

Exercise 18: 4e   Answer the following:

5a) Show the following as Disjoint Sets.

F = {apple, orange, lemon}   V = {Potato, turnip, parsnip}

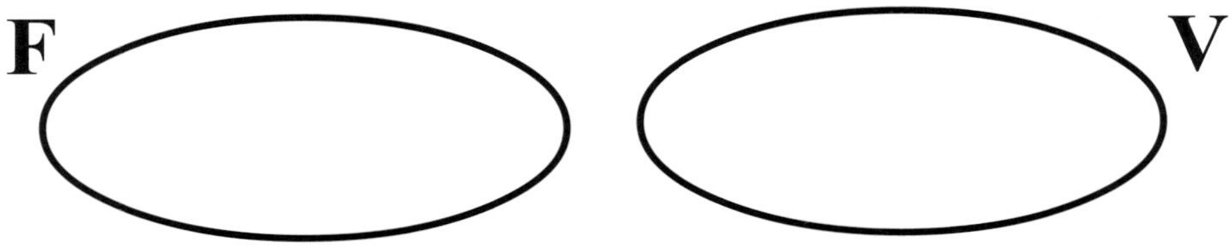

b) Show these Sets on the Venn Diagram.

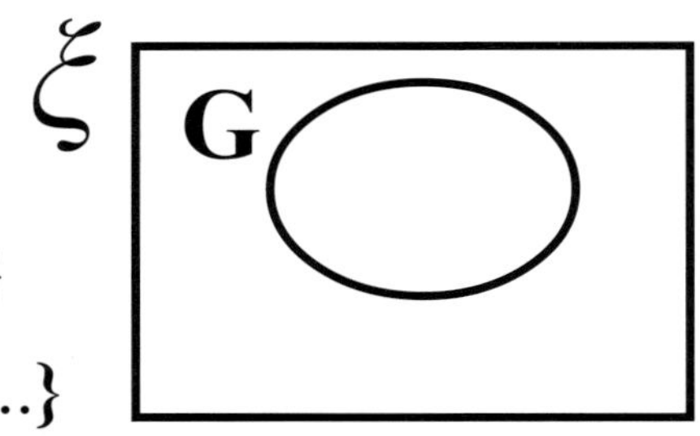

ξ = {I, V, X, D, M, Z}   G = {X, Z}

The Members of **G'** = {......................}

c) Show these Sets on the Venn Diagram below:

ξ = {1, 2, 3, 4, 5, 6, 7, 8, 9, 10, 11, 12, 13, 14, 15, 16}

R = {6, 8, 10, 12, 14, 15, 16}   S = {1, 4, 9, 16}

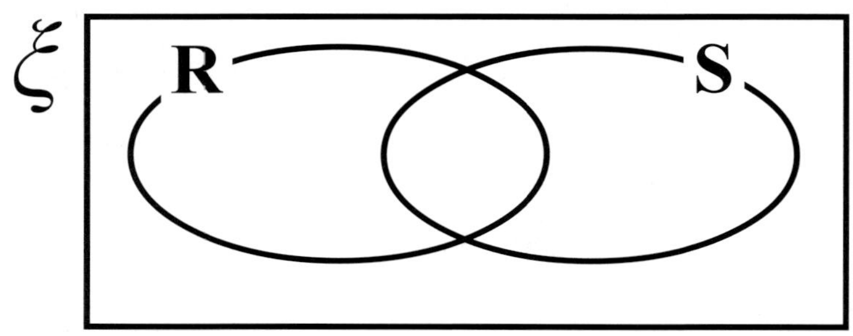

What are the Members of **R'**

{.......................

..........................}

d) Indicate these Sets on the Venn Diagram below:

ξ = {3, 4, 6, 8, 9, 12, 16, 18, 20, 21, 24, 28, 30, 32, 36}

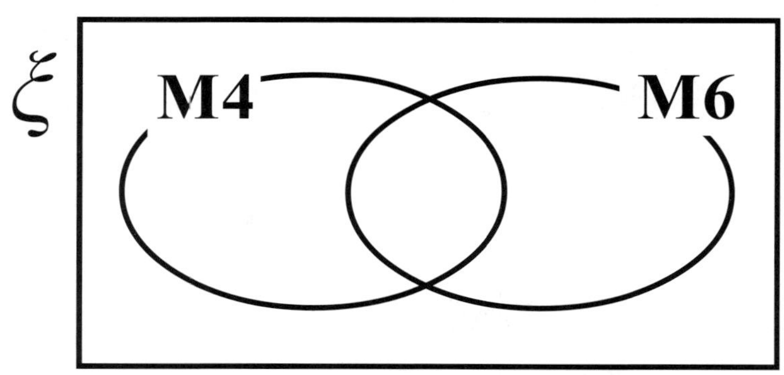

M4 = {4, 8, 12, 16, 20, 24, 28, 32, 36}

M6 = {6, 12, 18, 24, 30, 36}

e) Name the four Groupings for the following 12 Shapes on the Carroll Diagram below:

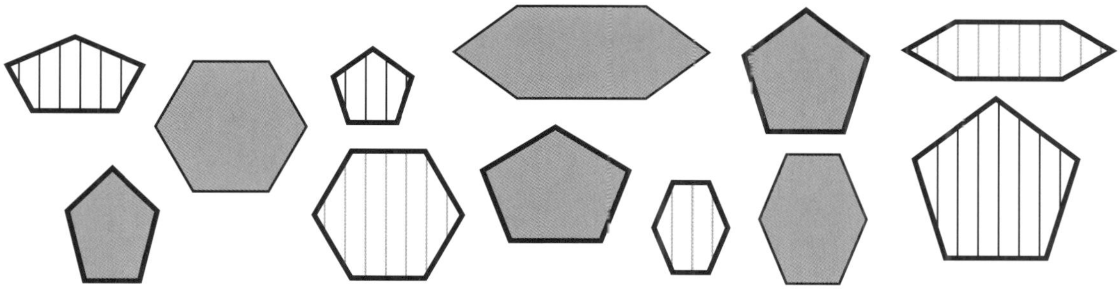

i) .... ii) ....

iii) ....

iv) ....

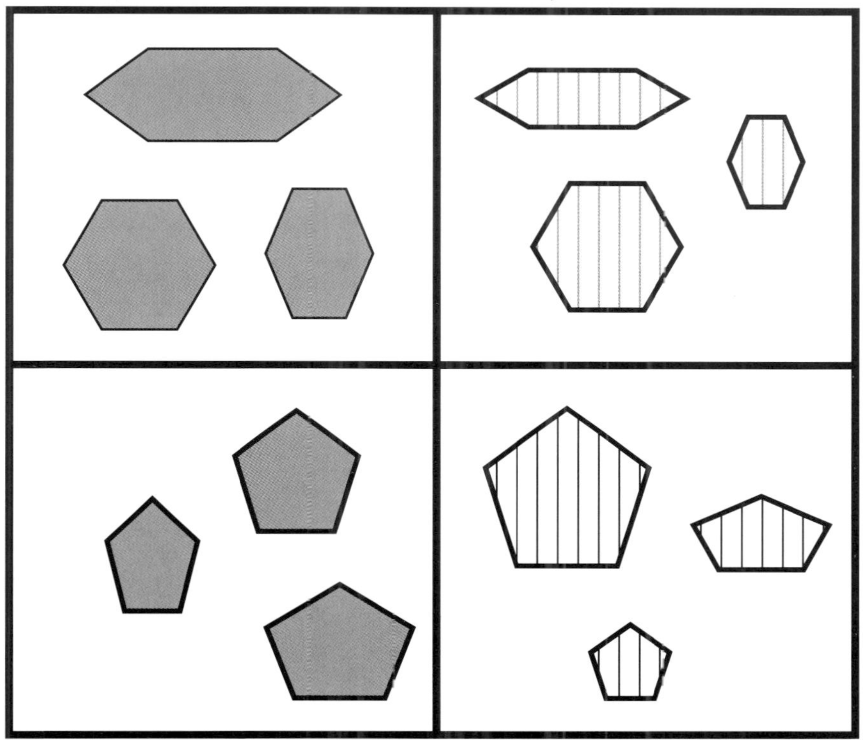

(vi). Using Venn Diagrams

Exercise 18: 4f Answer the following:

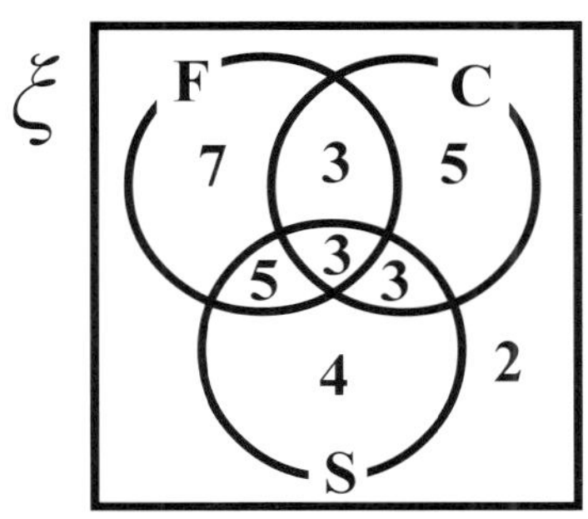

6a) Some children were asked whether they liked Films, Cartoons or Soaps.

What number liked all three? ....

How many liked soaps and films? ....

How many liked films? ....

There are .... children altogether.

F ∩ C = {........}   **F ∩ C ∩ S** = {........}

b) The diagram shows colour Relationships. Fill in the gaps using ∩ and ∪ or by inserting the subsets of the defined Relationship.

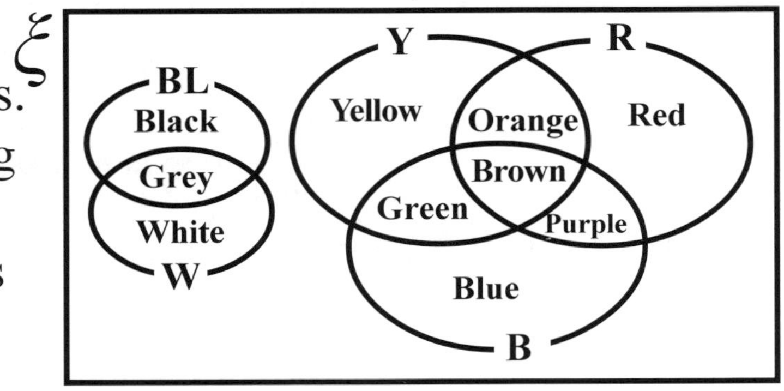

i) **BL ∩ W** = {..............} ii) **Y** ..... **B** = {green, brown}

iii) **Y** ..... **R** = {yellow, orange, green, brown, purple, red}

iv) **B ∪ R** = {............., ..., ..., ..., ..., ...}

---

c) A sports club Surveyed its members to see what activities they liked. **28** liked tennis, **20** liked squash and **27** liked football. Complete the Diagram.

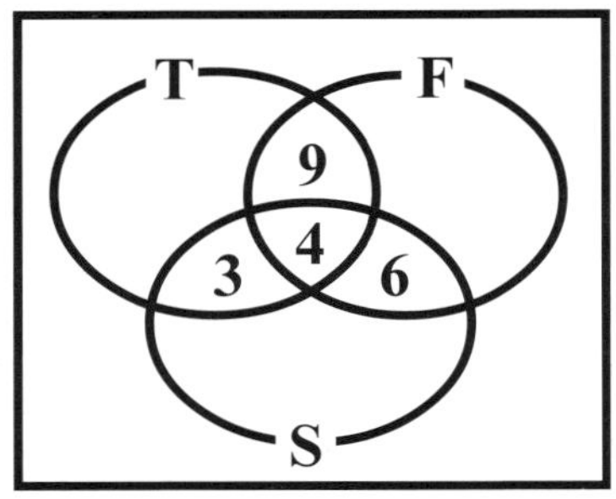

How many like:
tennis and squash? .... football and squash? ....
all three activities? .... football but not squash? ....

How many don't like:
squash? .... tennis? .... tennis or squash but like football? ....
How many people were Surveyed altogether? ....

d. Mappings

A Mapping (or Function) is a Connection between two Sets. Each first Set Member links with a second Set Member.

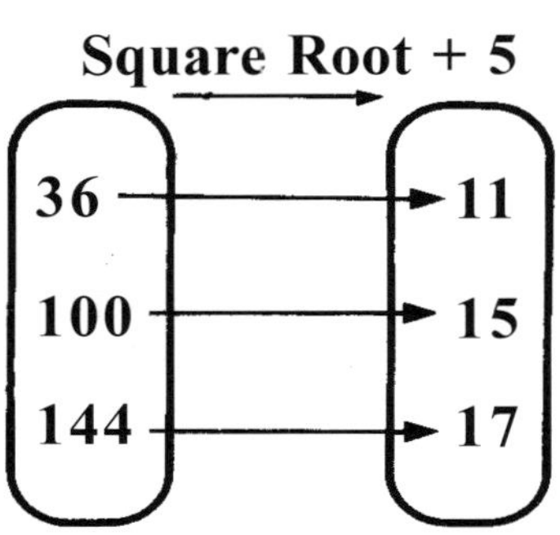

Map the numbers

Examples:

Note that Members of the first Set here have only one partner but the second Set can have more.

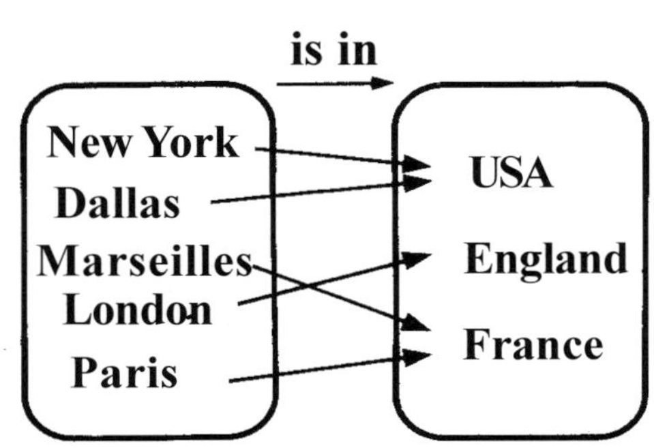

Map cities to countries

Mappings often make use of the Four Rules of Number. They can have two Operations. Test them out using: $+ \; - \; \times \; \div$

See also Mappings in Algebra (**See Book 6**).

Exercise 18: 4g Do the following Mappings:

7) Draw in the arrows for these Mappings:

a) **Divides exactly into** →

4	12
5	15
6	20
8	24

b) **is a multiple of** →

60	5
72	6
80	10
95	24

Write in the Mapping Rule above each Mapping:

c) .... →

- 12 → 1
- 15 → 2
- 24 → 5
- 30 → 7

d) .... →

- 3 → 14
- 7 → 22
- 10 → 28
- 20 → 48

Discover the Mapping Rule and write in the missing number:

e) →

- 3 → 16
- 6 → 25
- 7 → 28
- 11 → .....

f) →

- 4 → 6
- 7 → 12
- 11 → 20
- 24 → .....

e. Flow Diagrams

Flow Diagrams or Decision Trees provide a process for items to be Classified or Sorted into various Groups.

Example:

Make up a Decision Tree to help Stefan sort out a pile of hardback and paperback books.

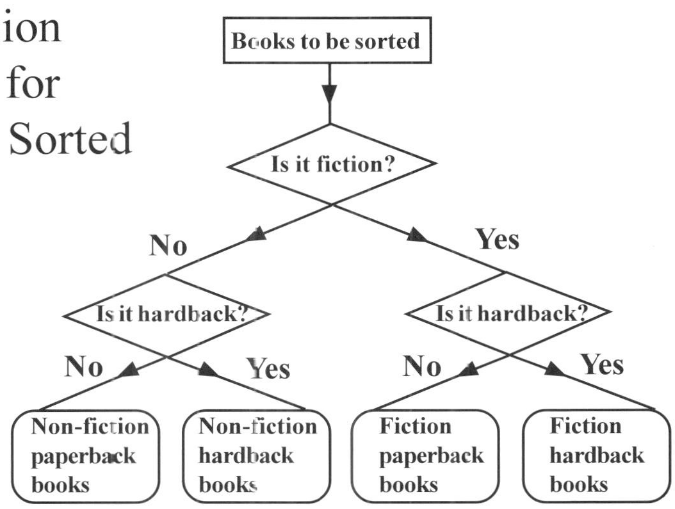

A Family Tree is another type of Flow Diagram.

Example:

This Family Tree shows three generations of the Noble family.
Question: Who is Mark's Grandmother?

Answer: Sally Noble

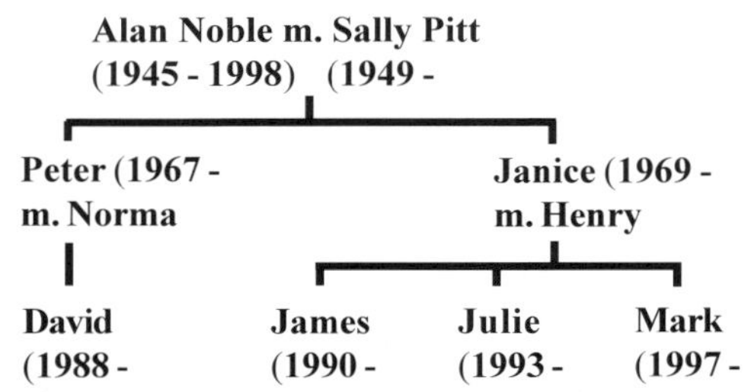

Exercise 18: 4h Answer the following:

8) a) Use the same Noble Family Tree (above) to answer:

i) How old was was David when his cousin Julie was born? .... yrs.

ii) Julie is Peter's .... iii) Mark is Sally's ....

iv) How old was James when his grandfather died? .... yrs.

---

b) A Flow Diagram is drawn to classify four metals.

i) Which metal is valuable and is yellow? ....

ii) Which metal is not valuable and not yellow? ....

iii) Brass is valuable, true or false? ....

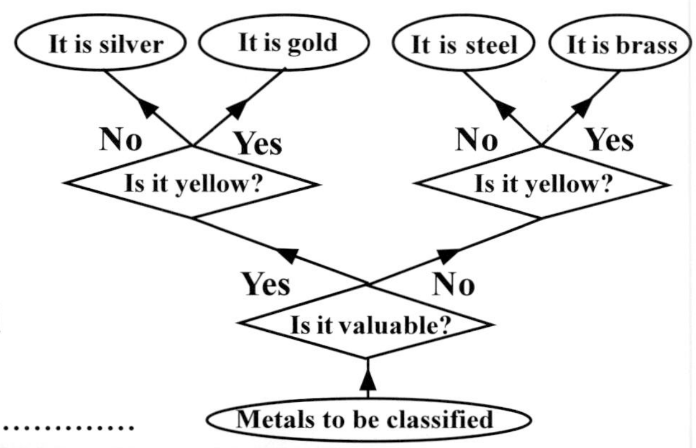

f. Stem and Leaf Diagrams

Stem and Leaf Diagrams are another way of recording information. Example:

The heights in cm of some children in a class are:
144, **162**, **150**, **154**, **158**, **167**, **130**, **132**, **143**
144, **143**, **152**. Show in a Stem and Leaf Diagram.

For the value **132cm** the stem is **13** and the leaf is **2**

13	0	2		
14	4	3	4	3
15	0	4	8	2
16	2	7		

To read off the values, multiply the Stem by 10 and add on the Leaf.

Stem = multiples of **10cm** so **162** becomes **16 | 2**

In a Stem and Leaf Diagram, the individual values are recorded. They can be read off the diagram.

13	0	2		
14	3	3	4	4
15	0	2	4	8
16	2	7		

The Data can be better organised by placing the Leaves in numerical order.

Exercise 18: 4i

Complete the Stem and Leaf Diagram below. Put the Leaves in numerical order.

9) The weights of some children in **kg** are:
32, **44**, **51**, **57**, **43**, **40**, **38**, **37**, **60**, **32**, **34**, **44**, **49**, **53**, **63**, **61**, **59**, **61**.

3	2	2	4	7	8
4					
5					
6					

g. Relational Diagrams

A Relational Diagram can help Solve a problem where things Relate to each other.
Example:

Paul is **7cm** taller than Lisa who is **12cm** shorter Barry. Who is the tallest?

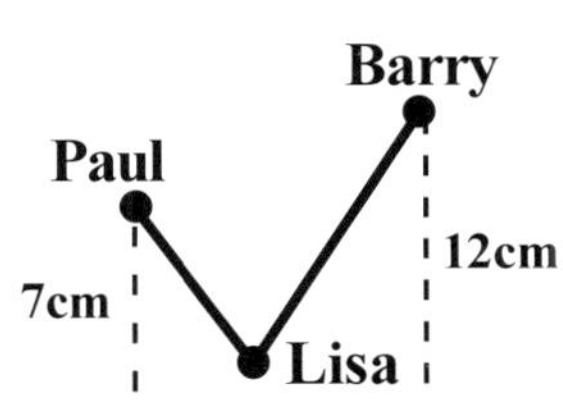

Answer: Barry is the tallest.

Exercise 18: 4j

10) a) **Six** years ago Pat was **3** years old. His father was **nine times** his age.
How old is his father now? .....
How old is Pat now? .....

b) In **3** years time John will be **twice** as old as his sister who is now **5**.
How old is John now?
.... years.

Score

6. Misleading Representations

Statistical information can sometimes be presented in a Misleading way through Charts, Graphs and Diagrams.
Example:

Give an example of a Misleading Bar Chart.

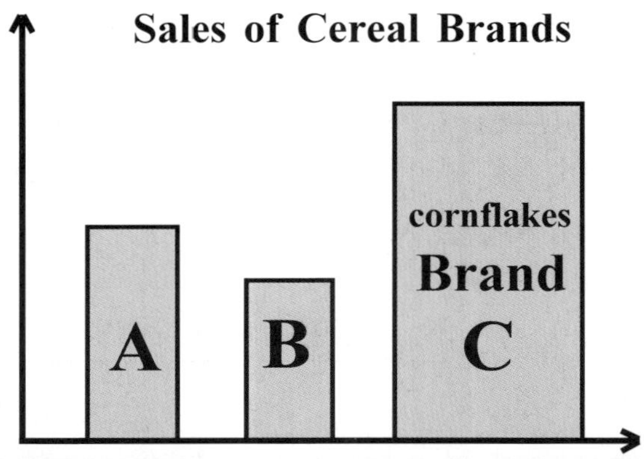

This Bar Chart is Misleading for 3 reasons:

1. No Scales are given.
2. The bars are not the same width.
3. The comparison is irrelevant, as no clear information is given about what type of cereals A and B actually are.

Exercise 18: 5 Give written answers to the following:

The results of children's tests in two school subjects were recorded over a six month period. What three things are Misleading about this Graph?

1) ....
....
....

2) ....
....
....

3) ....
....
....

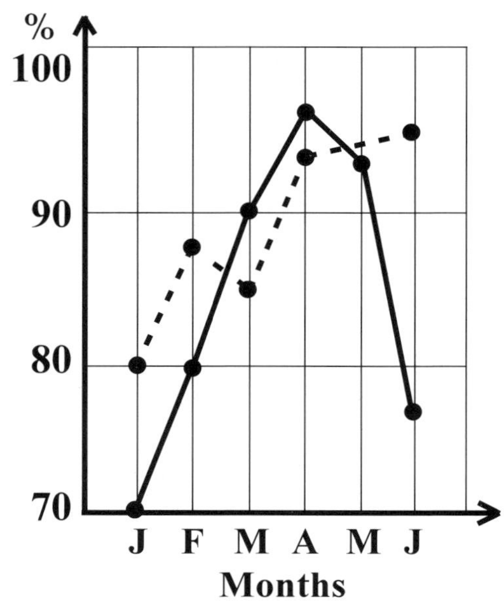

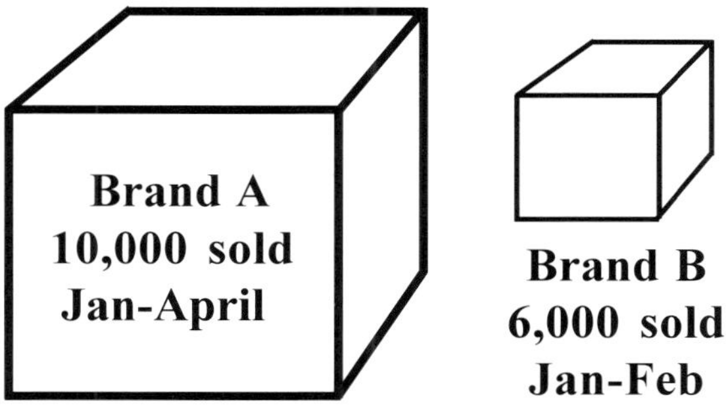

This Pictogram represents the sale of soap powders. What two things are Misleading about this Pictogram?

4) ....

....

5) ....

....

The Bar Chart shows the sale of chewing gum in 2005. What three things are Misleading about this Bar Chart?

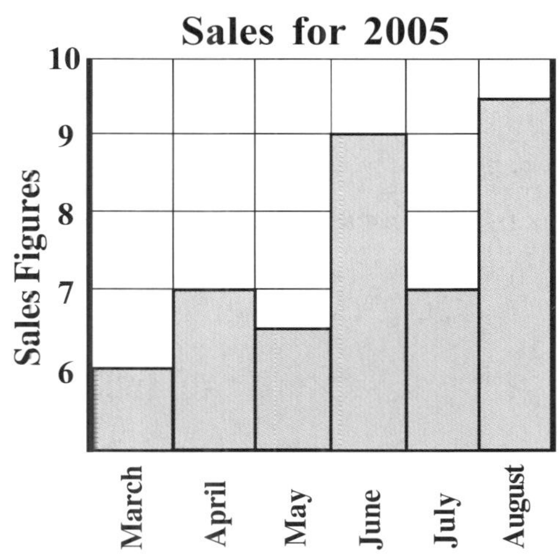

6) ....

....

....

7) ....

....

....

8) ....

....

....

The Pie Charts compare the Proportion of vehicles recorded on a road on two separate days. Give two reasons why they are Misleading.

Score

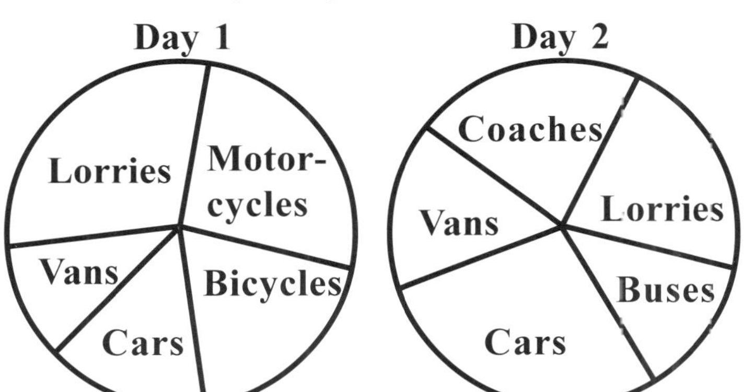

9) ....

....

....

....

10) ....

....

....

....

7. More Data Problems

Exercise 18: 6 Answer the following:

1) This Graph shows the number of CDs a shop sold over a **4 week** period.

   a) How many more CDs were sold in **week 2** than in week 3? .... CDs.

   b) How many CDs were sold in **week 2**? .... CDs.

   c) What were the total sales over the **four** week period? .... CDs.

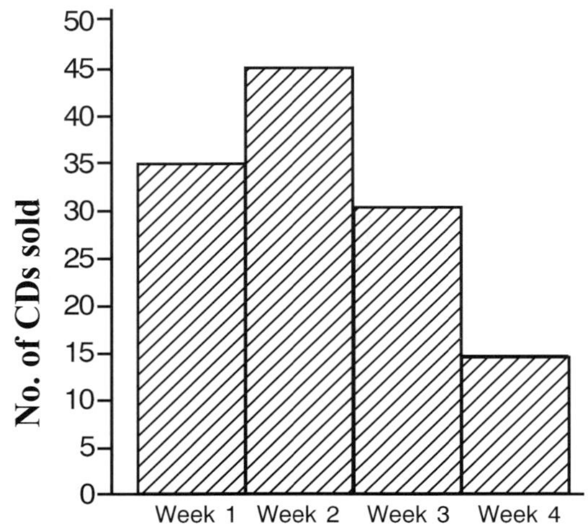

---

2) A group of children were Surveyed about the kind of homes they lived in. Some lived in detached houses; some lived in semi-detached houses; others lived in terraced houses and **6** lived in flats.

   a) How many children lived in terraced houses? ....

   b) How many children lived in detached houses? ....

   c) How many children lived in semi-detached houses? ....

   d) How many children were Surveyed altogether? ....

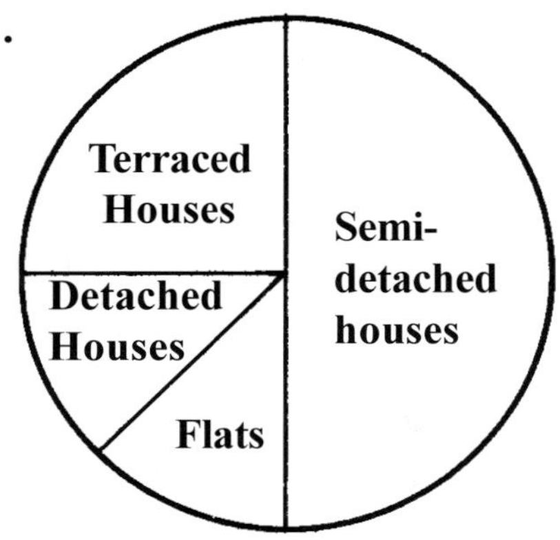

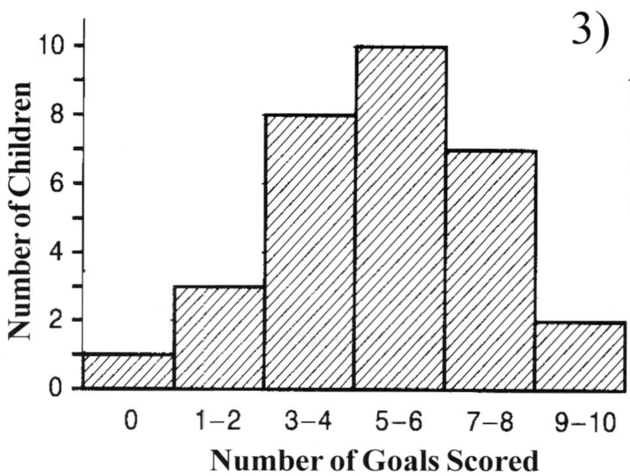

3) This Chart shows how many times some children from a youth club scored a goal in a penalty competition.

   a) How many children scored less than **5 times**? ....

   b) How many children scored at least **1 goal**? ....

   c) How many children scored more than **6 goals**? ....

4) Rajveer was ill for a week and his Temperature was Plotted on a Graph. The dotted Line shows the normal Temperature of a person.

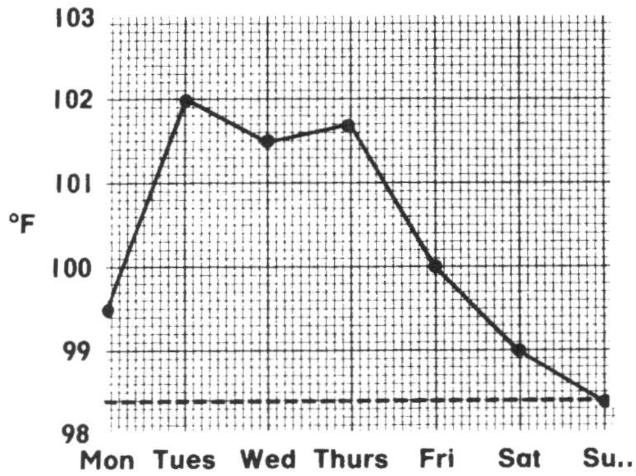

a) On what day was Rajveer most ill? ....

b) What is the normal Temperature of a person? .... °F

c) What was his Temperature halfway through the illness? .... °F

d) On what day did Rajveer start to get better? ....

---

5) The **6×**, **8×** and **9×** tables up to **72** were placed on a Venn Diagram. Fill in the numbers that Intersect on the Diagram.

What numbers Intersect on:

a) 6× and 8× table only ....

b) 6× and 9× table only ....

c) 8× and 9× table only ....

d) 6×, 8× and 9× table ....

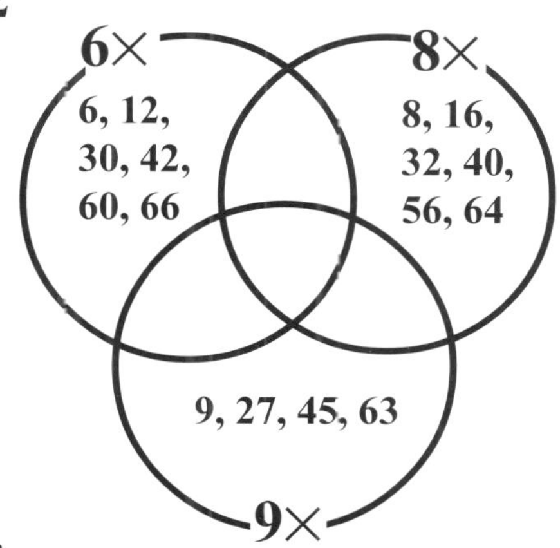

---

6) The Graph represents the journey Times of a car and a small aeroplane. The aeroplane got to the destination more quickly.

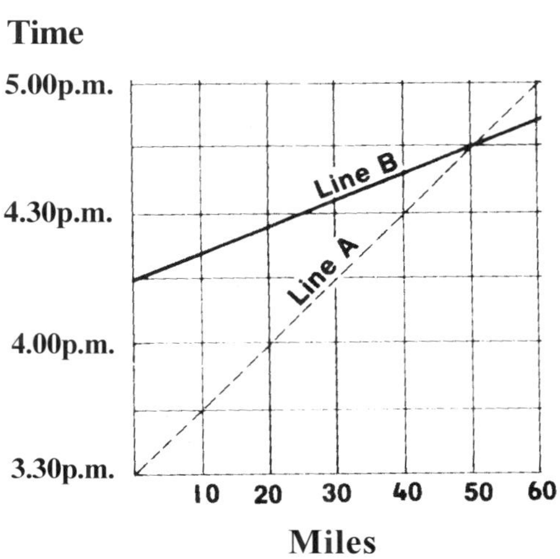

a) Which line represents the journey of the aeroplane? ....

b) When did the aeroplane overtake the car on its journey? .... p.m.

c) What was the car's Average Speed? .... mph.

d) What was the aeroplane's Average Speed? .... mph.

e) When did the car start its journey? .... p.m.

f) How many miles had the car gone before the aeroplane began its journey? .... miles.

Distances are given in km

London				
340	**Paris**			
2500	**2480**	**Moscow**		
5900	**6150**	**7800**	**New York**	
9500	**9600**	**7100**	**13000**	**Hong Kong**

7) This Table shows Distances in kilometres between five major airports in the world.

a) How much further is it from London to New York than from London to Moscow? .... km.

b) How far is it there and back from Paris to Hong Kong? .... km.

c) If a woman travelled from London to Hong Kong via <u>all</u> the airports in the sequence given, how far did she travel? .... km.

---

8) A school Survey was conducted on children's favourite colours. **36** children liked green, **21** liked yellow, **12** liked blue, **9** liked red and **30** liked other colours. Represent this on the Pie Chart.

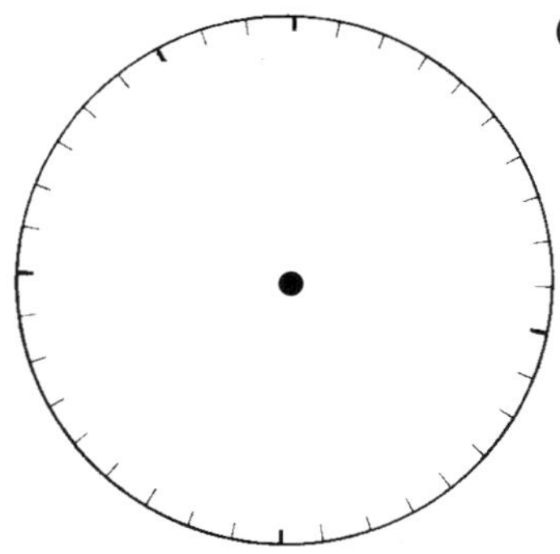

(The chart is divided into 36 Segments to help)

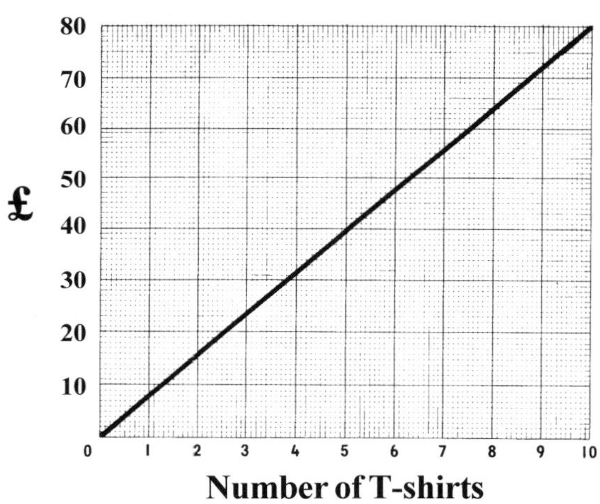

9) This Graph represents the price of T-shirts at a store.

a) **5** T-shirts cost £ ....

b) How many T-shirts could be bought for **£80**? ....

c) How much would it cost to buy **15** T-shirts? £ ....

d) How much would it cost to buy one T-shirt? £ ....

---

10) Paul sat a spelling test every day for a week.

a) What was Paul's Mean (Average) Score for the week? .... mks.

b) What was his Modal Score for the week? .... mks.

c) What was Median Score for the week? .... mks.

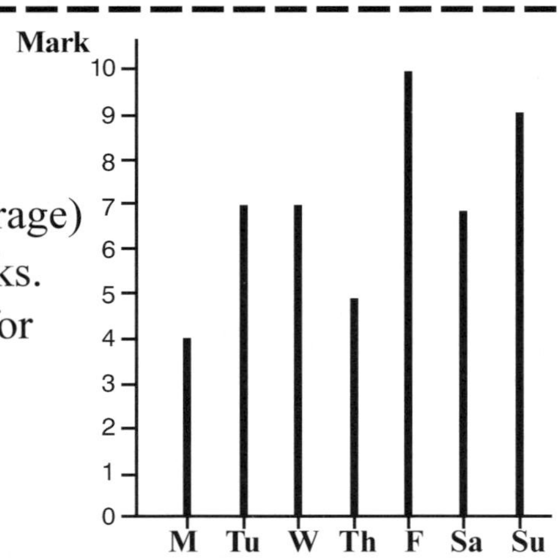

Score

Answers

Chapter Sixteen
Area, Perimeter & Volume

Exercise 16: 1a
1) 26cm 2) 14cm 3) 21cm

Exercise 16: 1b
4) 147cm 5) 72cm 6) 69m 7) 66m
8) 90m 9) 164mm 10) 150cm

Exercise 16: 2a
1) 35m^2 2) 14cm^2

Exercise 16: 2b
3) 6cm 4) 6m 5) 7cm

Exercise 16: 2c
6) 24m 7) 15cm^2 8) a) 5m b) 16m

Exercise 16: 2d
9) 46cm^2 10) 40m^2

Exercise 16: 3a
1) 17.5cm^2 2) 75cm^2 3) 12m^2

Exercise 16: 3b
4) 24mm 5) 9m 6) 3cm

Exercise 16: 3c
7) 27cm 8) 15m 9) 8cm
10) a) 250mm^2 b) 14cm c) 10m

Exercise 16: 4a
1) 13.5cm^2 2) 5cm 3) 3.5cm^2
4) 3mm 5) a) 150mm^2 b) 12cm c) 5m

Exercise 16: 4b
6) 18cm^2 7) 4 cm 8) 14cm
9) 5cm 10) 9 cm

Exercise 16: 5a
1) 50.24cm^2 2) 28.26cm^2
3) 39.25cm^2 4) 616mm^2 5) 1386m^2

Exercise 16: 5b
6) 25.12cm 7) 18.84cm
8) 15.7cm 9) 110mm 10) 176m

Exercise 16: 6a
1) 160.14cm^2 2) 452.16cm^2
3) 593.46m^2 4) 5.93cm^2 5) 100.48cm^2

Exercise 16: 6b
6) 91cm^2 7) 67cm^2 8) 96cm^2
9) 7,240mm^2 10) 150m^2

Exercise 16: 7
1) 0.4m^2 2) 200ha 3) 5cm^2
4) 200,000cm^2 5) 50,000m^2
6) 3cm^2 7) 3.2ha 8) a) 500ha
b) 750ha 9) a) 1.92m^2 b) 3.2m^2
10) 25,000cm^2

Exercise 16: 8a
1) 110cm^3

Exercise 16: 8b
2a) 240m^3 b) 100cm^3

Exercise 16: 8c
3) 6,000mm^3 4) 2,700cm^3

Exercise 16: 8d
5a) 1,280cm^3 b) 282m^3

Exercise 16: 8e
6a) 11m b) 7cm

Exercise 16: 8f
7a) 231m^3 b) 75cm^3

Exercise 16: 8g
8) 50.24cm^3

Exercise 16: 8h
9) 17.7kg 10) 0.8ℓ

Exercise 16: 9
1) 13,104m^2 2) 20 turns 3) 12m
4) 15m^3 5) A = 5m^2 B = 3m^2
C = 3m^2 6) a) 26m b) 29m
7) 3cm 8) 36cm^2 9) 40cm
10) A = 10.00cm^2 B = 7.50cm^2
C=6.25cm^2 D=4.81cm^2 E=3.44cm^2

Chapter Seventeen
Geometry

Exercise 17: 1a

1) 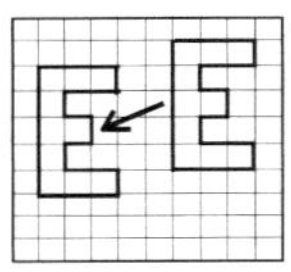 2) 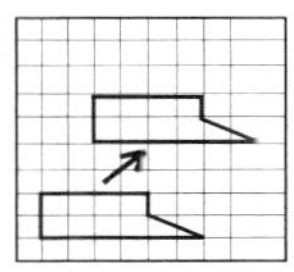

3) 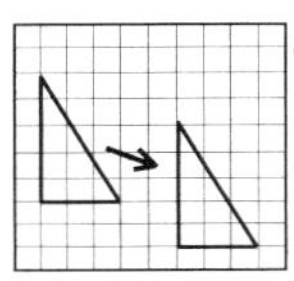 4) 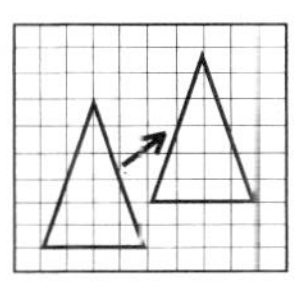

5) a) 5 squares down and 1 square left
b) 2 squares right and 3 squares up or 3 squares up and 2 squares right

Exercise 17: 1b

6) 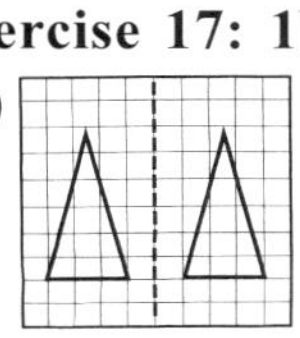 7) 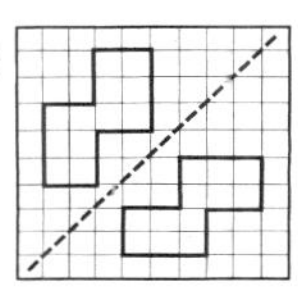

8) 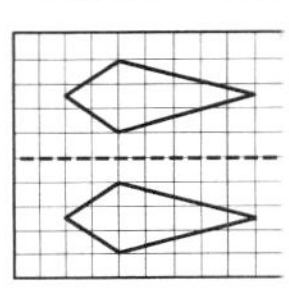 9) 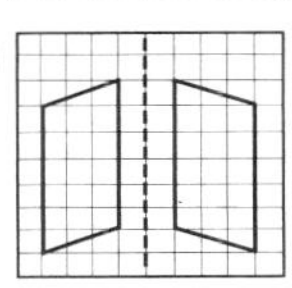

10) a) **True**/False b) True/**False**
c) True/**False**

Exercise 17: 2a
Shapes Rotated from A to B

1) 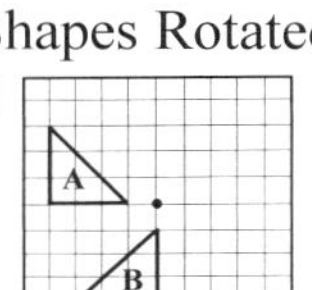

2) 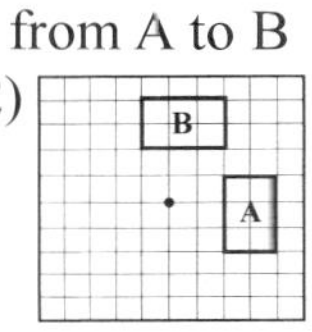

3) 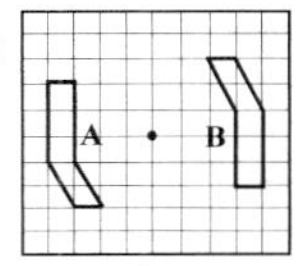

4) 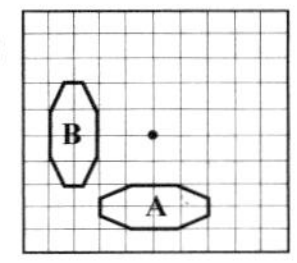

5) a) 270° b) Yes/**No**

Exercise 17: 2b
Shape A enlarged to shape B

6) 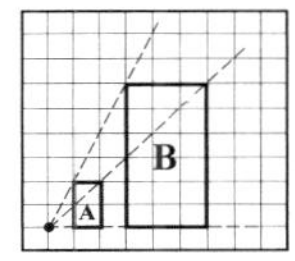

7) 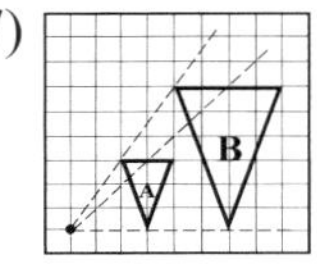

Exercise 17: 2c

8) 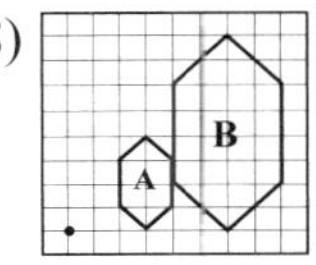

9) 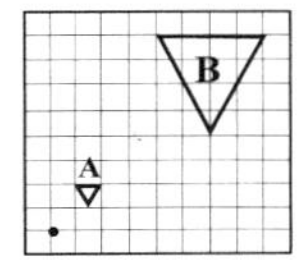

10) Scale Factor of:
a) 2 b) 4 c) 2

Exercise 17: 3
1) Yes 2) Yes 3) No
4) Yes 5) Yes 6) No
7) Yes 8) Yes 9) No 10) No

Exercise 17: 4
1) A & D 2) C & G
3) B, E & F 4) A 5) C
6) B 7) B 8) A, D & E
9) B & C 10) F

Exercise 17: 5a
1) Yes 2) No 3) No
4) Yes 5) Tessellates

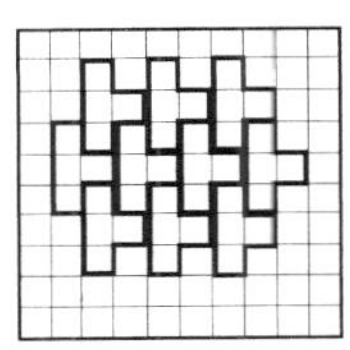 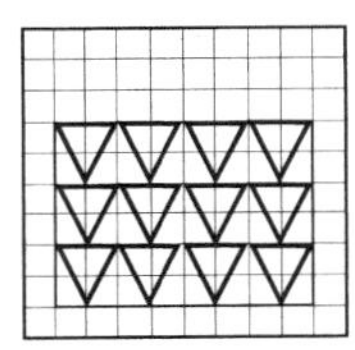

Exercise 17: 5b
6) No 7) Yes 8) Yes
9) a) 34 units b) Yes
10) a) 11 units b) 31 units

Exercise 17: 6a
1a) i) 0804 ii) 0608
iii) 0909 iv) v) vi) below

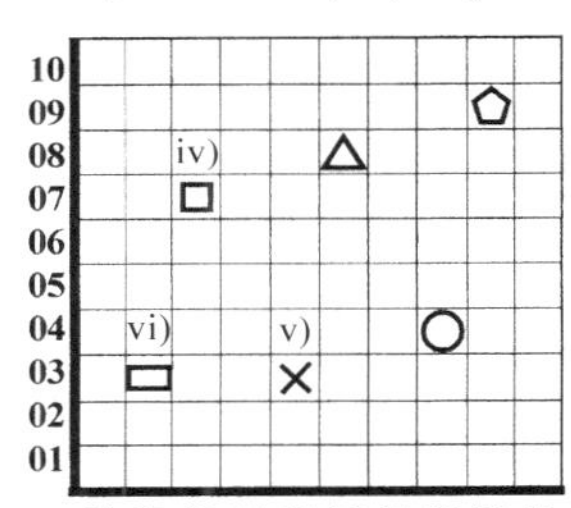

1b) i) Wreck - C,2
ii) Rocks - I,7
iii) Forest - F,3
iv) Treasure - H,2

Exercise 17: 6b

2) a) Parallelogram
b) Isosceles Triangle

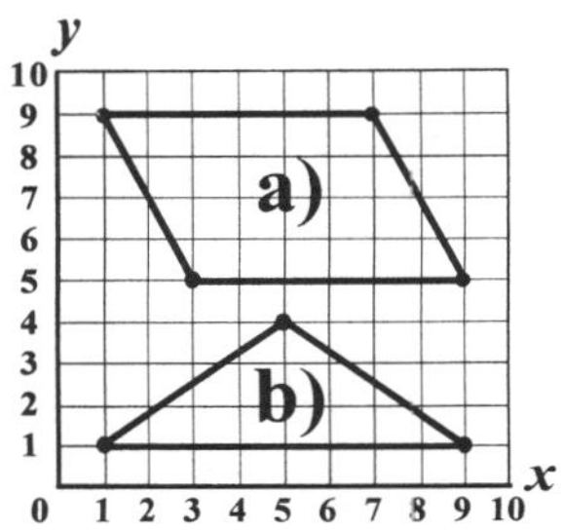

3) a) A = (2, 7); B = (3, 9)
C = (6, 9); D = (7, 7)
E = (6, 5); F = (3, 5)
b) G = (2, 1); H = (8, 4)
I = (8, 1)

4) a) A = (1, 8); B = (3, 9)
C= (4, 5); D = (3, 1)
E = (1, 2)

b)

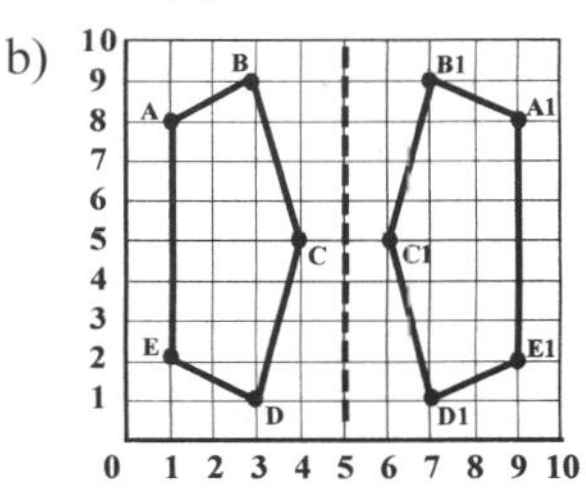

A1 = (9, 8); B1 = (7, 9)
C1 = (6, 5); D1 = (7, 1)
E1 = (9, 2)

5) a) trapezium b) rectangle

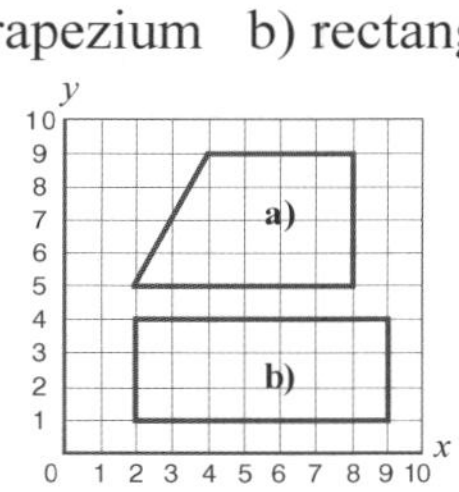

6a) A = (1, 7) B = (3, 9)
C = (9, 9) D = (7, 7)
E = (9, 5) F = (3, 5)
6b) G = (2, 2) H = (9, 4)
I = (8, 1)
7a) A = (1, 8) B = (4, 9)
C = (2, 5) D = (4, 1)
E = (1, 2)
7b) A1 = (9, 8) B1 = (6, 9)
C1 = (8, 5) D1 = (6, 1)
E1 = (9, 2)

Exercise 17: 6c

8a) i) Square ii) Irregular Hexagon
iii) Isosceles Trapezium

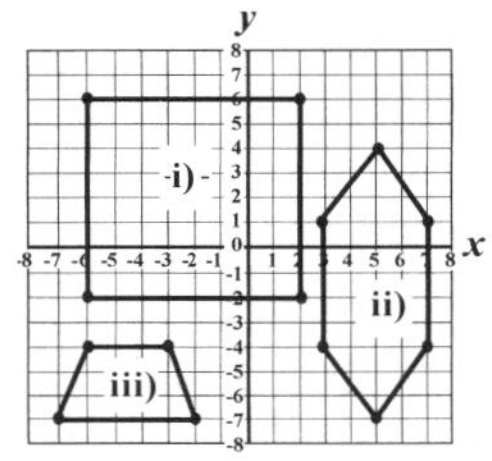

8b) i) pentagon ii) parallelogram
iii) scalene triangle

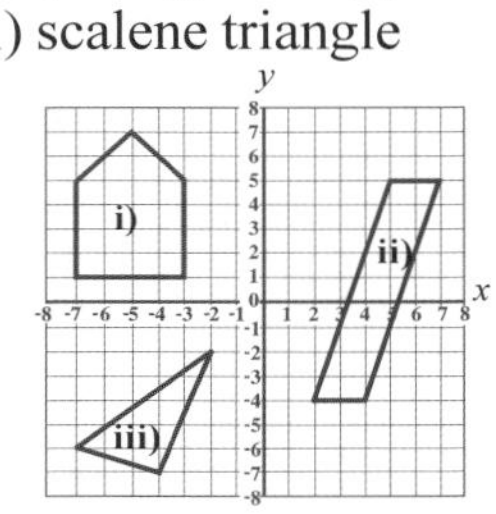

8c) i) A = (-6, 5) B = (-4, 6)
C = (-1, 1) D = (-4, -2)
E = (-6, -1) F = (-7, 3) Decagon
ii) G = (6, 5) H = (1, -5) Diagonal
iii) I = (-7, -7) J = (3, -7) Horizontal
iv) K = (6, 2) L = (6, -7) Vertical
v) Perpendicular

9a) a = (-5, -2); b = (-2, -2)
c = (-5, -6); d = (-2, -6)
9b) a = (4, -7); b = (2, -2); c = (6, -2)

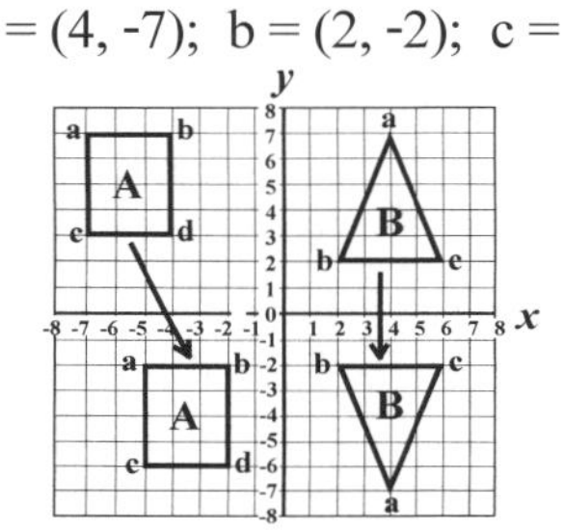

Exercise 17: 6d

10a) Forward 2, Turn left,
Forward 1, Turn right,
Forward 3, Turn right,
Forward 2, Turn left,
Forward 2, Turn right,
Forward 3.

10b) Turn right 45°, Forward 4m,
Turn right 45°, Forward 6 m,
Turn right 45°, Forward 4m,
Turn right 135°, Forward 8m.

Chapter Eighteen
Tables, Charts, Graphs and Diagrams

Exercise 18: 1a

1) a) 15 b) 37 2) a) 2
b) Nadia & Rohit c) Class 4

Exercise 18: 1b

3) a) 330 miles b) 620 miles
c) 250 miles d) 3,300 miles

Exercise 18: 1c

4) a) 2 girls b) Anne
c) 1 girl d) Anne, Delia
5) a) City E b) 2 cities c) City F

Exercise 18: 1d

6) a = 26; e = 32; i = 25;
o = 10; u = 3

Exercise 18: 1e

7)

Times	Tally	Fr
1-15	𝍸 𝍸	10
16-30	𝍸	5
31-45	𝍸 𝍸	10
46-60	𝍸	5

Exercise 18: 1f

8)

Times (t)	Tally	Fr
$0 \le t < 5$	𝍸	5
$5 \le t < 10$	𝍸 IIII	9
$10 \le t < 15$	IIII	4
$15 \le t < 20$	IIII	4

9)

Weight (w)	Tally	Fr
$35 \le w < 40$	𝍸 IIII	9
$40 \le w < 45$	𝍸 IIII	9
$45 \le w < 50$	III	3
$50 \le w < 55$	III	3
$55 \le w < 60$	𝍸 I	6

Exercise 18: 1g

10) a) Mean = 2.27;
Median number = 2
b) Mean = 3; Range = 4

Number of children at each table	Frequency (Number of tables)	Total number of children for table sittings
1	3	$1 \times 3 = 3$
2	5	10
3	5	15
4	3	12
5	4	20
Totals	20	60

Exercise 18: 2a

1) a) Wed b) 8 hrs c) 42 hrs d) 6 hrs

2)

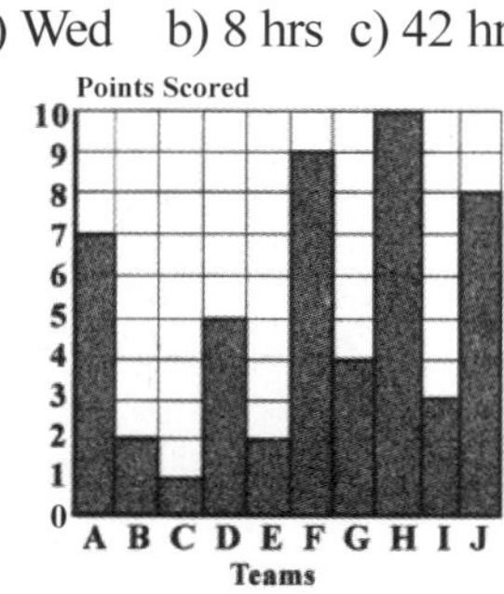

3) a) 18 b) 13 c) False

Exercise 18: 2b

4) a) Red - 5 b) Green - 5
c) Blue - 5 d) Mauve - 10
e) 40 children

Answers

5) a) $\frac{1}{4}$ liked cartoons

b) 12 liked sitcoms

c) $12\frac{1}{2}$% liked soaps

d) Game Shows - 135°

6)

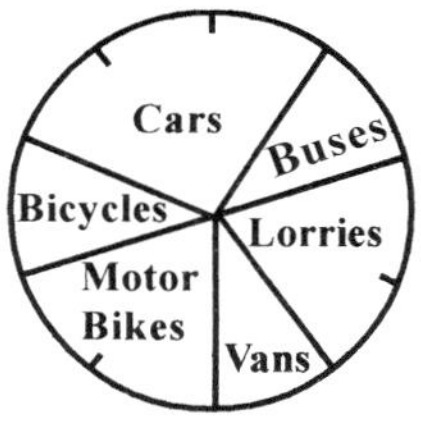

7) a) 27 cars b) 90 vehicles

c) 30 vehicles per hour

Exercise 18: 2c

8)

Pet	Fr.	Angle
Rabbit	12	144°
Cat	4	48°
Dog	2	24°
Hamster	9	108°
Budgie	3	36°
Total	**30**	**360°**

9)

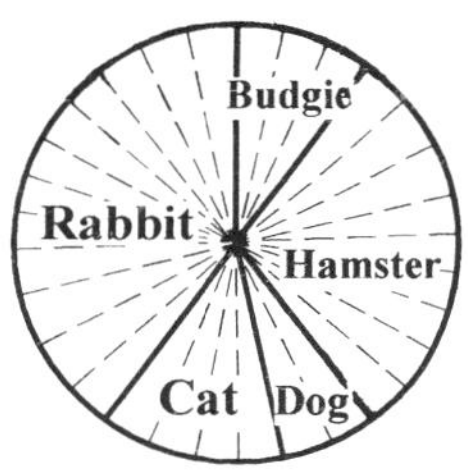

10)

Candidate	Fr.	Angle
Jonathan	8	144°
Jaspreet	5	90°
Paula	7	126°
Total	**20**	**360°**

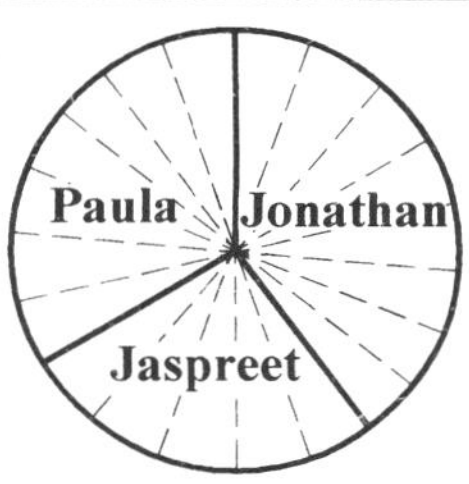

Exercise 18: 3a

1) a)

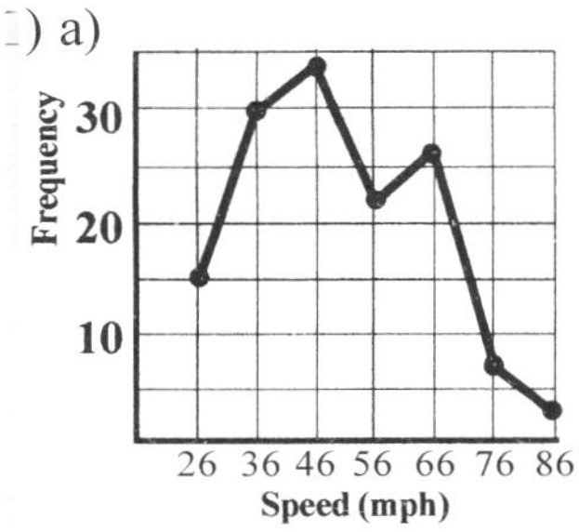

b) 136 vehicles c) 58 vehicles

2)a)

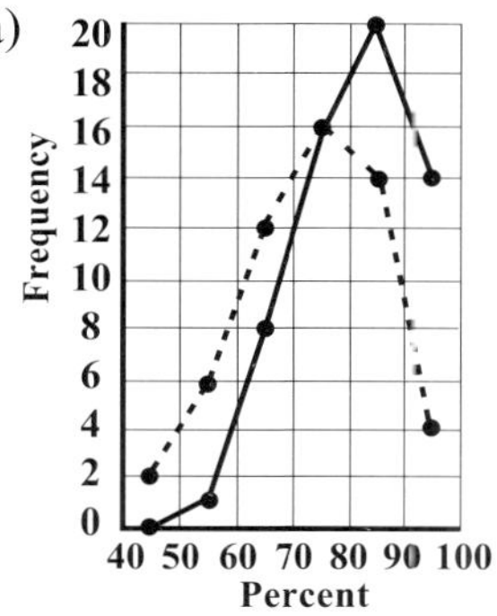

b) 71-80% c) Maths

Exercise 18: 3b

3) a) 60km = 40 miles

b) 200 miles = 300km

4) a) 4lbs = 2kg b) 3.5kg = 7.5lbs

Exercise 18: 3c

5) a) 25mph b) 75mph

c) 150miles d) 37.5mph

6) a) Sanjay's line. (See below.)

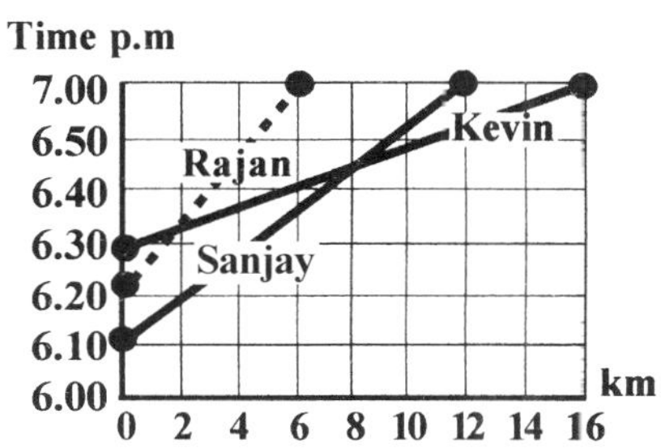

b) Rajan's journey c) 16km

d) 32km/hr e) 6.45p.m

Exercise 18: 3d

7) Scatter Graph plotted

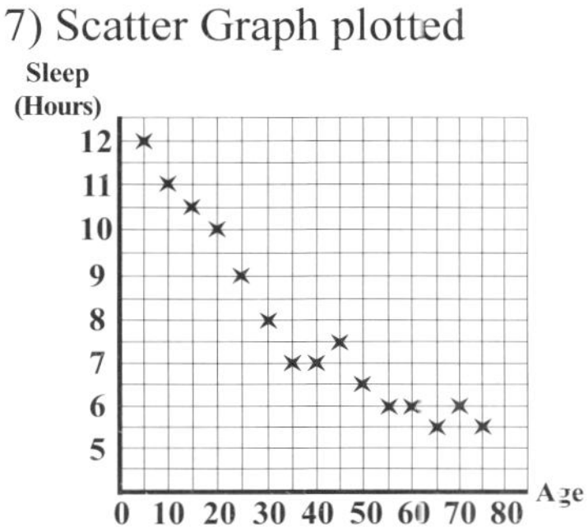

8) This is a Negative Correlation.

9) Scatter Graph plotted.

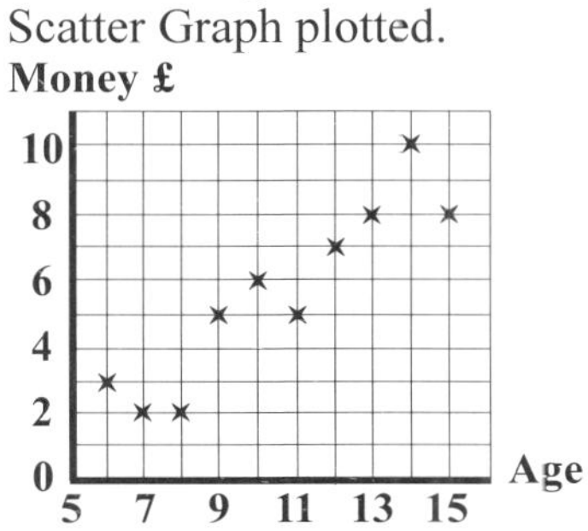

Yes Older children usually get more pocket money.

10) a) Moderate Positive

b) No Correlation

c) Strong Negative

Exercise 18: 4a

1) a) 50 b) Thurs c) 140

Exercise 18: 4b

2a) T = {Triangles}

2b) C = {Colours}

2c) P = {Planets}

2d) A = {Factory Apples}

2e) W = {Monday, Tuesday Wednesday, Thursday, Friday, Saturday, Sunday; n(W) = 7

2f) January, June, July; n(J) = 3

2g) P = {} or Ø; n (P) = 0

2h) ∞ set or infinite/endless set

2i) Apple ∈ = {Fruit}

Pea ∉ = {Fruit}

Lamb ∈ = {Meat}

Pear ∉ = {Vegetable}

Beef ∉ = {Fruit}

Pork ∈ = {Meat}

2j)

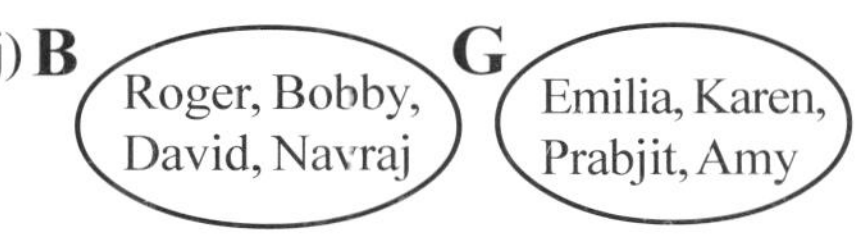

Exercise 18: 4c

3a) E ⊄ F R ⊄ N or R ⊃ N

T ⊄ F T ⊄ D R ⊂ T

3b) Subsets {Paul, Darren, Akash} {Paul, Darren}, {Paul, Akash} {Darren, Akash}, {Paul}, {Darren}, {Akash}, {}.

Subsets {2, 4, 6, 8}, {2, 4, 6} {2, 6, 8}, {2, 4, 8}, {4, 6, 8}, {2, 4}, {2, 6}, {2, 8}, {4, 6}, {4, 8}, {6, 8}, {2}, {4}, {6}, {8}, {}

3c)

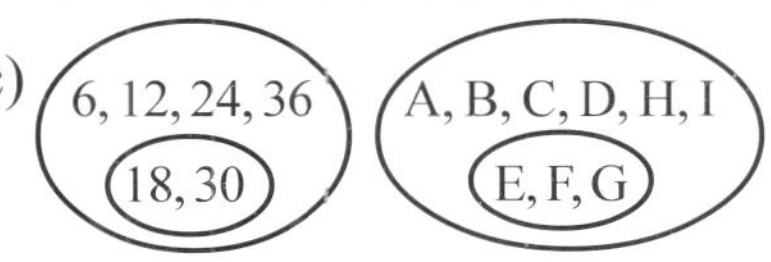

Exercise 18: 4d

4a) A cap B or A ∩ B = {4, 16, 36}

A cup B or A ∪ B = {1, 4, 8, 9, 12, 16, 20, 24, 25, 28, 32, 36}

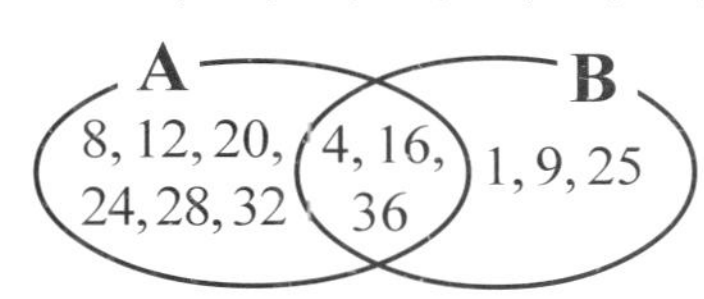

4b) A ∩ B = {bishop};
A ∩ C = {knight, bishop, castle}
B ∩ C = {bishop, priest}
A ∩ B ∩ C = {bishop}
A ∪ B ∪ C = {knight, bishop, castle, pawn, priest, vicar, dean, maiden, chivalry}

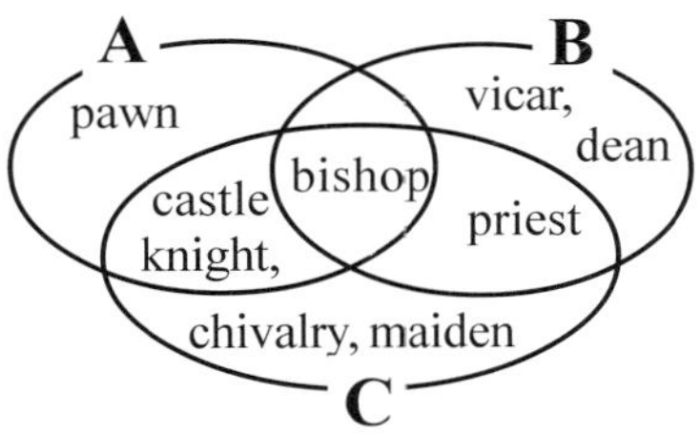

4c) A ∩ B = {a, e, u};
A ∩ C = {o, u}
B ∩ C = {u, v, w}
A ∩ B ∩ C = {u}
A ∪ B ∪ C = {a, b, c, d, e, i, n, o, p, q, r, s, t, u, v, w, x, y, z}

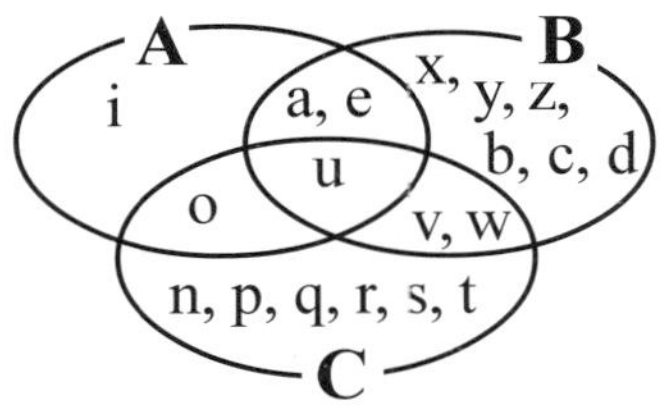

Exercise 18: 4e

5a)

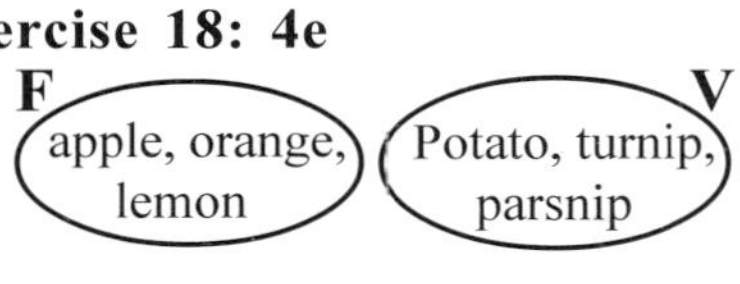

5b)

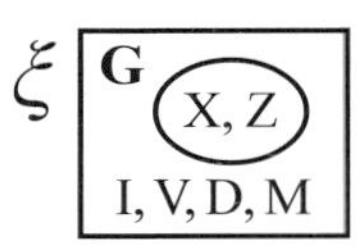

G' = {I, V, D, M}

5c)

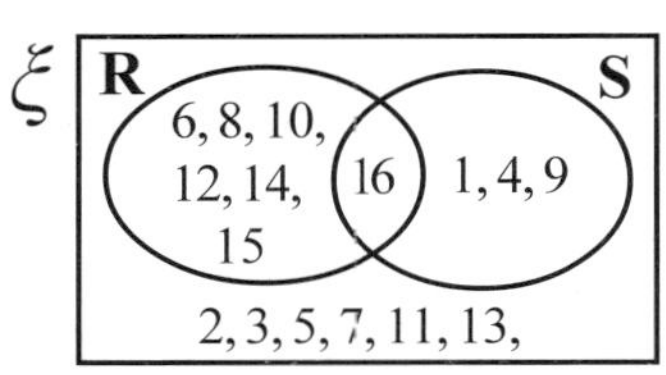

R' = {1, 2, 3, 4, 5, 7, 9, 11, 13}

5d)

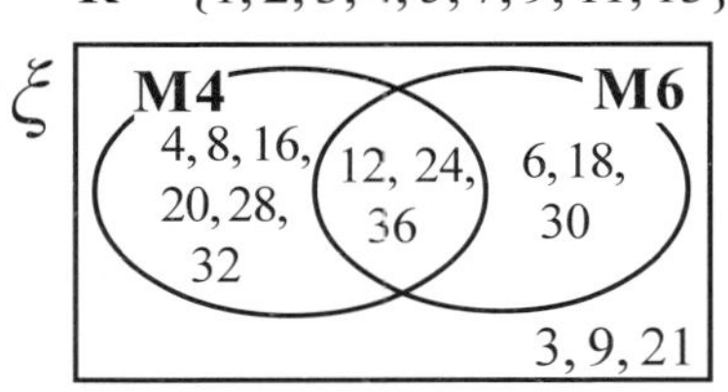

5e) i) grey ii) striped or shaded
iii) hexagonal iv) pentagonal

Exercise 18: 4f

6a) i) 3 ii) 8 iii) 18 iv) 32
v) F ∩ C = {6} vi) F ∩ C ∩ S = {3}

6b) i) Grey ii) Y ∩ B iii) Y ∪ R
v) {green, brown purple, orange, red, blue}

6c) i) 7 ii) 10 iii) 4 iv) 17
v) 29 vi) 21 vii) 8 viii) 49

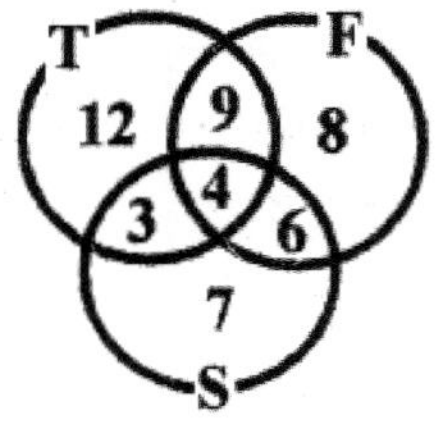

Exercise 18: 4g

7) a)

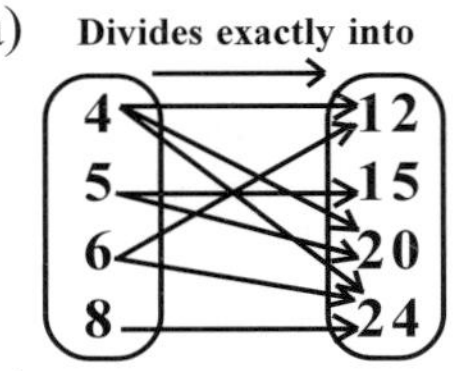

b)

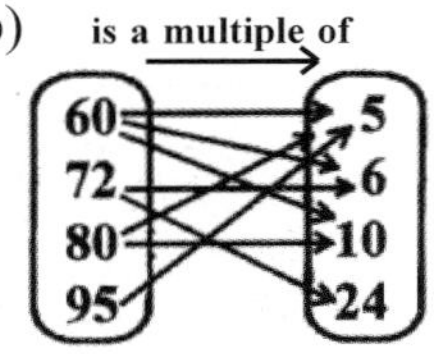

c) Minus 9, divide by 3 or Divide by 3, minus 3
d) Multiply by 2, plus 8 or Plus 4, multiply by 2
e) Rule is Multiply by 3, plus 7 Answer = 40
f) Rule is Multiply by 2, minus 2 or Minus 1, multiply by 2 Answer = 46

Exercise 18: 4h

8) a) i) 5 yrs ii) niece
iii) grandson iv) 8 yrs
b) i) Gold ii) Steel iii) False

Exercise 18: 4i

9)

3	2	2	4	7	8
4	0	3	4	4	9
5	1	3	7	9	
6	0	1	1	3	

Exercise 18: 4j

10) a) Father is 33 years Pat is 9 years b) 13 years

Exercise 18: 5

1) The graph does not begin at zero, so we have no idea how the class performed before this time.
2) No indication is given as to what subjects are actually being compared.
3) No information is given about the number of children being tested.
4) Brand A did not sell more than twice as much as Brand B, but its volume gives the impression it sold even more than this.
5) Sales of each brand took place over different time periods.
6) The graph does not begin at zero. We do not know what happened before this period.
7) The Graph is supposed to represent 2003, but only six months are shown.
8) No indication is given whether the sales figures represent single packs, hundreds or thousands.
9) The Pie Charts do not represent all the same vehicles.
10) There is no information about the number of vehicles.

Exercise 18: 6

1) a) 15 b) 45 c) 125
2) a) 12 b) 6 c) 24 d) 48
3) a) 12 b) 30 c) 9
4) a) Tues b) 98.4° F
c) 101.7° F d) Thurs

5)

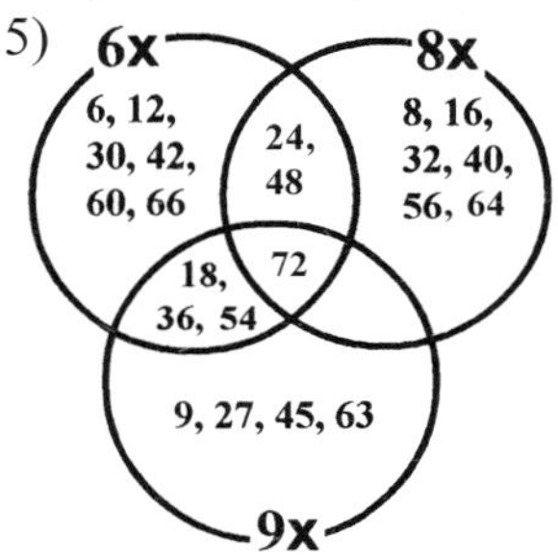

a) 24, 48 b) 18, 36, 54
c) None d) 72
6) a) Line B b) 4.45p.m
c) 40mph d) 100mph
e) 3.30p.m f) 30miles
7) a) 3,400km b) 19,200km
c) 23,620km
8)

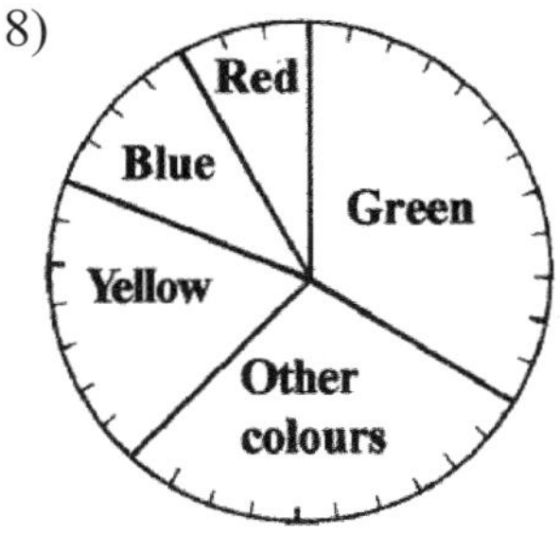

9) a) £40 b) 10 T-shirts
c) £120 d) £8
10) a) 7 mks b) 7 mks c) 7 mks

PROGRESS CHARTS

16. PERIMETER, AREA & VOLUME

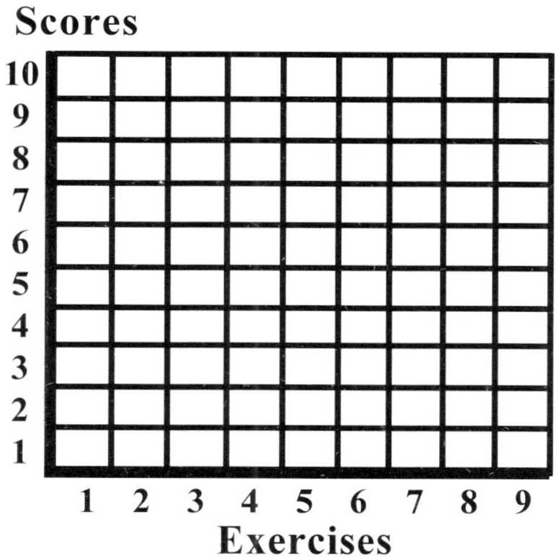

Total Score

Percentage

%

17. GEOMETRY

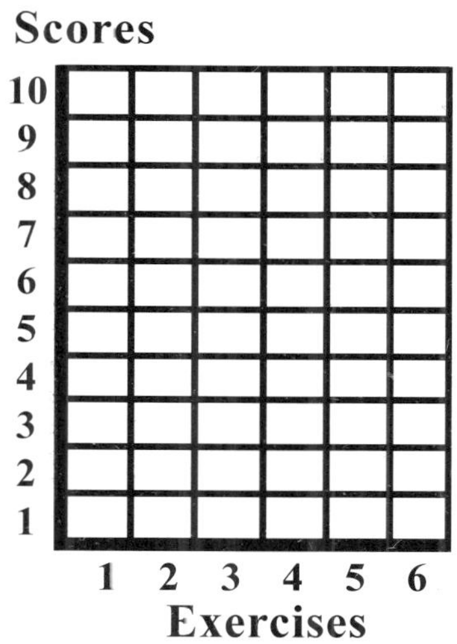

Total Score

Percentage

%

18. TABLES, CHARTS, GRAPHS & DIAGRAMS

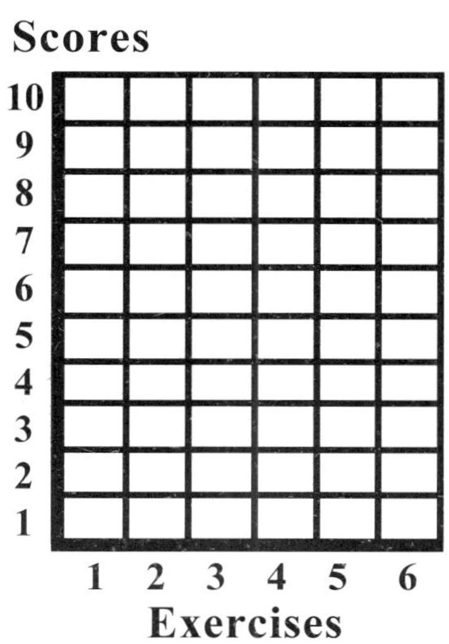

Total Score

Percentage

%

For the average add up % and divide by 3

Overall Percentage

%

CERTIFICATE OF ACHIEVEMENT (Fifth)

This certifies.................................

has completed **Maths Book Five** *successfully.*

Overall Percentage Score Achieved. %

Comment...

....

Signed ....

(teacher/parent/guardian)

Date ....